SUMMER · WINTER

CHICKEN

LORI LONGBOTHAM

Photography by

MELANIE ACEVEDO

QUILL

WILLIAM MORROW AND COMPANY

NEW YORK

Library of Congress Cataloging-in-Publication Data
Longbotham, Lori.
Summer / winter chicken / Lori Longbotham.
p.   cm.
ISBN 0-688-15212-0
1. Cookery (Chicken)   I. Title.
TX750. C45L66   1997
641.6'65--dc21
97-6247
CIP

ISBN: 0-688-15212-0

Editor: DEBORAH MINTCHEFF
Designer: SUSI OBERHELMAN
Assistant Editor: SARAH STEWART
Assistant Designer: AYAKO HOSONO
Food Stylist: KEVIN CRAFTS
Prop Stylist: ROBYN GLASER

First Edition

1   2   3   4   5   6   7   8   9   10

PRODUCED BY SMALLWOOD & STEWART, INC., NEW YORK CITY

PRINTED IN SINGAPORE

SUMMER CHICKEN
CONTENTS

CHICKEN

SUMMER

INTRODUCTION

During the warm weather, I want to spend as little time as possible in the kitchen. I'm interested in light, simple meals quickly put together with the season's abundance of fresh produce. Chicken, it turns out, is perfect for this style of cooking. Not only is it easy to prepare, but it is also a perfect partner for all that I love about summer food—sweet basil, juicy ripe cherries, local raspberries, just-picked sweet corn, succulent peaches, garden-fresh tomatoes.

What follows are my favorite chicken salads and sandwiches, picnics, and grills, all perfect for summer eating. I've borrowed liberally from around the world—a Thai chicken salad, an Italian-style panini, chicken quesadillas from Mexico, Caribbean jerk chicken, classic American barbecued chicken—all as easygoing, refreshing, and unpretentious as the season itself.

CHANGING SEASONS: HOW TO USE THIS BOOK

When you feel like moving on to winter dishes, just flip the book over and you'll find a whole new set of recipes for cold-weather comfort. Each half is a mini book unto itself, complete with its own page numbers and index.

CHICKEN
SUMMER

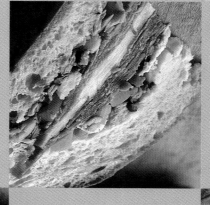

CHICKEN CAESAR SALAD

GARLIC CROUTONS

¼ cup fruity olive oil

2 garlic cloves, halved lengthwise

¼ teaspoon salt

¼ teaspoon freshly ground pepper

3 cups ¾-inch cubes French bread

ANCHOVY DRESSING

4 anchovy fillets, or to taste, rinsed

4 garlic cloves

2 teaspoons tarragon vinegar

2 teaspoons fresh lemon juice

1 teaspoon Worcestershire sauce

½ teaspoon dry mustard

½ cup extra-virgin olive oil

4 boneless skinless chicken breast
    halves (about 5 ounces each)

2 tablespoons extra-virgin olive oil

Salt & freshly ground pepper

4 heads romaine lettuce, outer
    leaves reserved for another
    use, pale-green inner leaves
    washed, dried & torn into bite-
    size pieces (about 12 cups)

Parmesan cheese shavings
    (removed with a vegetable
    peeler)

CAESAR SALAD IS ON JUST ABOUT EVERY TRENDY
RESTAURANT MENU, PREPARED WITH EVERYTHING FROM
SQUID TO ROASTED VEGETABLES. I THINK
SOME OF THESE OFFERINGS ARE STRETCHING THE POINT
A BIT, BUT I LOVE THIS CLASSIC VERSION
WITH THE ADDITION OF GRILLED CHICKEN BREASTS.

Prepare the garlic croutons: Preheat the oven to 350°F. Heat the oil, garlic, salt, and pepper in a small saucepan over medium heat until hot. Remove from the heat and let stand for 10 minutes; discard the garlic. In a large bowl, toss the bread cubes with the garlic oil. Spread the bread in a single layer on a baking sheet. Bake, shaking the pan occasionally, for 12 to 15 minutes, or until golden brown. Set aside.

Preheat a grill to hot and brush with oil or preheat a grill pan.

Prepare the anchovy dressing: With a large knife, mince the anchovies and garlic to a paste. In a small bowl, whisk together the anchovy mixture, vinegar, lemon juice, Worcestershire sauce, and mustard. Add the oil in a slow stream, whisking until smooth and thick. Set aside.

On a large plate, drizzle the chicken with the oil and season with salt and pepper. Grill the chicken for 5 to 7 minutes on each side, or until browned and cooked through. Transfer to a cutting board, and when cool enough to handle, cut the chicken breasts diagonally into thin strips.

In a large bowl, combine the romaine, chicken, croutons, and dressing. Transfer to serving plates and top with the Parmesan shavings.

Serves   4

WHEN ASKED HOW LONG SHE SOAKED HER CHICKEN
IN BUTTERMILK, MY TEXAS GRANDMOTHER SAID, "JUST AS
LONG AS IT TAKES ME TO GO TO CHURCH."
I FIGURE SHE WAS GONE FOR ABOUT THREE HOURS, SO
THAT'S HOW LONG I MARINATE MY CHICKEN.

½ cup buttermilk

½ lemon, thinly sliced

2 scallions, minced

2 tablespoons each minced
    jalapeño chile, fresh cilantro
    & peeled fresh ginger

1 teaspoon minced garlic

2 whole chicken breasts, split &
    each cut into 3 pieces

BUTTERMILK DRESSING

¼ cup buttermilk

2 tablespoons vegetable oil

1 teaspoon each minced jalapeño
    chile & peeled fresh ginger

½ teaspoon grated lemon zest

1 teaspoon fresh lemon juice

1 teaspoon Dijon mustard

½ teaspoon minced garlic

Salt & ground red pepper

Vegetable oil, for frying

½ cup all-purpose flour

1 teaspoon each salt & ground
    red pepper

8 cups mixed salad greens

Halved cherry tomatoes, for garnish

In a large bowl, mix the buttermilk, lemon slices, scallions, jalapeño, 1 tablespoon of the cilantro, the ginger, and garlic. Add the chicken and turn to coat. Cover and marinate in the refrigerator for 3 hours.

Meanwhile, prepare the buttermilk dressing: In a small bowl, whisk together the buttermilk, oil, jalapeño, ginger, lemon zest, lemon juice, mustard, and garlic, and season with salt and ground red pepper, whisking until smooth. Cover and refrigerate until ready to serve.

Heat ¾ inch of oil in a large skillet over medium-high heat until hot but not smoking. Meanwhile, place the flour on a large plate and combine with the salt and ground red pepper. Lightly coat the chicken breasts with the flour, shaking off the excess.

Fry the chicken, in batches, for about 8 to 10 minutes on each side, or until deep golden brown and cooked through. Remove the chicken to a large paper towel–lined plate.

Briefly whisk the dressing. In a large bowl, toss the mixed greens with the dressing, and transfer to serving plates. Place the hot chicken on top and arrange the cherry tomatoes on the side. Sprinkle with the remaining 1 tablespoon cilantro and serve.

Serves 4

RASPBERRIES AREN'T JUST FOR DESSERT
ANYMORE. VINAIGRETTES CONTAINING RASPBERRY VINEGAR
HAVE BEEN AROUND FOR QUITE A LONG TIME,
AND YOU'LL FIND THAT USING BOTH THE VINEGAR AND THE
FRUIT INCREASES THE PLEASURE GEOMETRICALLY.
THIS STUNNING SALAD IS DELICIOUS, AND IT MAKES A
GREAT SUMMERTIME MAIN COURSE.

RASPBERRY VINEGARETTE

2 shallots, minced

1½ tablespoons raspberry vinegar

1½ teaspoons fresh thyme leaves

1 teaspoon Dijon mustard

Salt & freshly ground pepper

¼ cup fruity olive oil

4 boneless skinless chicken breast halves (about 5 ounces each)

10 cups mesclun or other mixed salad greens

½ pint fresh raspberries

Prepare the raspberry vinaigrette: In a small bowl, whisk together the shallots, vinegar, thyme, and mustard, and season with salt, and pepper. Add the oil in a slow stream, whisking constantly until smooth and thick.

Place the chicken on a large plate and drizzle with 2 tablespoons of the vinaigrette, turning to coat. Cover and marinate in the refrigerator for about 1 hour, turning occasionally.

Preheat a grill to hot and brush with oil, or place a stovetop grill pan over medium heat.

Grill the chicken for 5 to 7 minutes on each side, or until golden brown and cooked through. Transfer to a plate and set aside.

In a large bowl, toss the mesclun with the dressing and about half the raspberries. Transfer to serving plates and place the chicken on top of the greens. Garnish with the remaining raspberries and serve.

CHICKEN & ORZO SALAD WITH RADISHES

Serves 4

1 whole chicken breast
(about 1 pound)

¼ pound snow peas, cut into
¼-inch-wide diagonal slices

1 cup orzo (rice-shaped pasta)

1 cup 1-inch-long diagonal slices
pencil-thin asparagus
(6 to 8 ounces)

½ cup diced yellow
bell pepper (¼-inch)

½ cup diced red onion (¼-inch)

6 radishes, halved & thinly sliced

2 tablespoons fruity olive oil

2 tablespoons fresh lemon juice,
or more to taste

2 tablespoons each minced fresh
flat-leaf parsley, mint &
snipped chives

1 teaspoon grated lemon zest

Salt & freshly ground pepper

HERE'S A NEAT TRICK: PUT THE SNOW PEAS IN A COLANDER AND THEN DRAIN THE PASTA OVER THEM—THE BOILING WATER COOKS THE PEAS JUST RIGHT, AND SINCE THE ASPARAGUS COOKS IN THE WATER WITH THE PASTA, THERE'S NO NEED FOR A SEPARATE POT. IF YOU'RE NOT SERVING THIS SALAD RIGHT AWAY, TASTE IT JUST BEFORE SERVING. THE ORZO REALLY SOAKS UP THE LEMON JUICE, SALT, AND PEPPER.

Put the chicken into a large saucepan, add enough cold water to cover, and bring to a boil over high heat. Reduce the heat and simmer for 15 minutes. Remove the saucepan from the heat and set aside for 20 minutes. Drain the chicken and when cool enough to handle, finely shred the meat, discarding the skin and bones.

Place the snow peas in a colander in the sink. Cook the orzo in a large saucepan of boiling salted water according to the package directions, until just tender, adding the asparagus to the pot for last 2 minutes of cooking. Drain the orzo in the colander, rinse under cold running water until cool, and drain well.

Transfer the orzo, snow peas, and shredded chicken to a large serving bowl. Add the remaining ingredients, season with salt and pepper, and toss until well combined. Serve immediately, or refrigerate and serve cold.

TARRAGON CHICKEN SALAD WITH MELON

Serves 4

THIS REFRESHING SUMMERY SALAD IS BEST
SERVED AS SOON AS IT'S MADE. IF THE RED ONION IS TOO
STRONG, IT WILL OVERPOWER THESE COOL
DELICATE FLAVORS; SOAK THE CHOPPED ONION IN A BOWL
OF ICE WATER FOR ABOUT FIFTEEN
MINUTES, DRAIN, AND BLOT DRY ON PAPER TOWELS—
THE HARSHNESS WILL BE GONE.

1 whole chicken breast (about 1 pound)

½ cup minced red onions

3 tablespoons olive oil

3 tablespoons fresh lime juice, or to taste

1 tablespoon minced fresh tarragon

2 cups diced honeydew melon (½-inch), plus thin slices, for garnish

1 cup thinly sliced seeded English cucumber

Salt & freshly ground pepper

1 large bunch arugula, trimmed & washed

Put the chicken into a large saucepan, add enough cold water to cover, and bring to a boil over high heat. Reduce the heat and simmer for 15 minutes. Remove from the heat and set aside for 20 minutes. Drain the chicken and when cool enough to handle, finely shred the meat, discarding the skin and bones.

In a large bowl, whisk together the onions, oil, lime juice, and tarragon. Stir in the chicken, diced honeydew, and cucumber, and season with salt and pepper.

To serve, arrange the arugula leaves on a serving platter, spoon the chicken salad on top, and garnish with the honeydew slices.

THAI-STYLE CHICKEN SALAD

2 whole chicken breasts
(about 2¼ pounds)

¼ cup canola or other vegetable oil

¼ cup fresh lime juice

1 tablespoon Thai fish sauce
(nam pla)

2 teaspoons soy sauce

1½ teaspoons sugar

¼ teaspoon each crushed red
pepper flakes & freshly
ground pepper

2 bunches watercress, tough
stems discarded

1 cup each fresh mint &
cilantro leaves

2 small red onions, very thinly sliced

6 radishes, halved & thinly sliced

1 tablespoon very finely shredded
lemon zest

THAI FOOD IS ONE OF MY FAVORITE CUISINES.
THE INTENSITY OF THE FLAVORS AND THE MIX OF SWEET,
SOUR, SALTY, BITTER, AND HOT IN
ALMOST EVERY DISH IS THRILLING. THIS IS NOT A
TRADITIONAL THAI RECIPE, BUT THE
FLAVORS ARE DEFINITELY THAI. AS LONG AS YOU HAVE
FISH SAUCE ON HAND, YOU CAN MAKE THIS
DISH ANYTIME WITH GROCERIES FROM THE SUPERMARKET.

Put the chicken into a large deep skillet, add cold water to cover, and bring to a boil over high heat. Reduce the heat and simmer for 15 minutes. Remove from the heat and set aside for 20 minutes. Drain and when the chicken is cool enough to handle, finely shred the meat, discarding the skin and bones.

In a small bowl, whisk together the oil, lime juice, fish sauce, soy sauce, sugar, red pepper flakes, and pepper until smooth. Set aside.

In a large bowl, toss the watercress, mint, cilantro, onions, radishes, and lemon zest together.

Add the chicken and lime juice dressing to the watercress mixture, tossing to mix. Transfer the chicken salad to serving plates and serve.

TAKE-OUT CHICKEN & MANGO SALAD

1 cup cold water

¼ teaspoon curry powder

½ cup couscous

¼ cup diced red onion (¼-inch)

2 tablespoons fresh cilantro leaves, plus whole sprigs, for garnish

1 tablespoon olive oil

2 teaspoons rice vinegar

Salt & freshly ground pepper

3 cups mesclun or other mixed salad greens

1 small store-bought roasted chicken (about 2 pounds), cut into quarters

1 small ripe mango, peeled, pitted & cut into ½-inch dice

NEED DINNER IN A HURRY? ON YOUR WAY HOME FROM WORK, GRAB A ROAST CHICKEN AND A BAG OF WASHED GREENS. TAKE A MINUTE TO BOIL WATER FOR COUSCOUS, ADD A MANGO, AND YOU'VE GOT A VERY QUICK, VERY EASY DINNER WITH TROPICAL FLAVORS.

In a small saucepan, bring the water and curry powder to a boil over high heat. Add the couscous and onion, stir, and remove from the heat. Cover and let stand for 5 minutes.

Fluff the couscous with a fork and stir in the cilantro, 1 teaspoon of the oil, and 1 teaspoon of the vinegar. Season with salt and pepper.

In a large bowl, toss the mesclun with the remaining 2 teaspoons oil, the remaining 1 teaspoon vinegar, and season with salt and pepper.

To serve, place the greens on serving plates, top with the warm couscous mixture, and place the chicken quarters on the side. Scatter the mango over the top, and garnish with the cilantro sprigs.

DAGWOOD SANDWICH

DAGWOOD IS A COMIC STRIP CHARACTER
WHO'S BEEN AROUND A LONG TIME—HIS MAJOR CLAIMS
TO FAME ARE HIS LAZINESS AND THE HUGE
SANDWICHES HE EATS. SINCE WE'RE NUTRITION-CONSCIOUS
THESE DAYS, THIS SANDWICH IS A
HEALTHFUL ONE. IF YOU'D LIKE TO MAKE IT
HEALTHIER STILL, USE LOW-FAT
OR NONFAT MAYONNAISE AND TURKEY BACON.

4 boneless skinless chicken breast halves (about 5 ounces each)

1 tablespoon minced fresh flat-leaf parsley

1 tablespoon fruity olive oil

Salt & freshly ground pepper

12 slices bacon, halved crosswise

¾ cup mayonnaise, plus additional, for spreading

3 scallions, minced

½ teaspoon grated lemon zest

12 slices brioche or other bread, toasted if desired

¾ cup mesclun or 6 small romaine leaves

6 plum tomatoes, sliced

Preheat a grill to hot and brush with oil or place a stovetop grill pan over medium heat.

On a large plate, sprinkle the chicken with 1 teaspoon of the parsley and drizzle with the oil, turning to coat. Season with salt and pepper. Grill the chicken for 5 to 7 minutes on each side, or until golden brown and cooked through. Remove from the grill and when cool enough to handle, finely shred the chicken.

Cook the bacon, in batches, in a large skillet just until crisp. Drain on a paper towel–lined tray.

In a large bowl, combine the chicken, the remaining 2 teaspoons parsley, the mayonnaise, scallions, and lemon zest, and season with salt and pepper. Spread a small amount of mayonnaise on each slice of bread. Place the mesclun on 6 of the bread slices and top with the tomatoes, bacon, and chicken salad. Cover with the remaining bread and press down gently. Cut each sandwich in half and serve.

SANDWICHES   15

CHICKEN MUFFULETTA

Serves 4

DIRECT FROM NEW ORLEANS, THIS LUSCIOUS SANDWICH IS PRONOUNCED "MOO-FA-LETTA." AT THE CENTRAL GROCERY IN THE FRENCH QUARTER (THE FAVORED SPOT IN THE CITY FOR THIS SANDWICH), THEY MAKE IT WITH LOTS OF GARLIC. HERE YOU'RE GIVEN A RANGE. CHICKEN IS NOT A TRADITIONAL INGREDIENT, BUT MAYBE IT SHOULD BE.

OLIVE SALAD

1 cup finely chopped celery, including some leaves

1 cup drained giardinièra (Italian mixed pickled vegetables), chopped

1 cup pitted green & black brine-cured olives, chopped

½ cup fruity olive oil

¼ cup minced fresh flat-leaf parsley

1 to 4 garlic cloves, minced

Freshly ground pepper

2 boneless skinless chicken breast halves (about 5 ounces each)

One 10-inch round loaf country-style bread, split

¼ pound each thinly sliced smoked ham, provolone cheese & Genoa salami

Prepare the olive salad: In a medium-size bowl, combine the celery, giardinièra, olives, oil, parsley, garlic, and pepper to taste and toss until well mixed. Cover and marinate in the refrigerator overnight.

Preheat a grill to hot and brush with oil or place a stovetop grill pan over medium heat.

On a large plate, drizzle the chicken with some of the oil from the olive salad, turning to coat. Grill the chicken for 5 to 7 minutes on each side, or until browned and cooked through. Remove from the grill and when cool enough to handle, cut into thin diagonal slices.

Remove some of the doughy center of the bread to make room for the filling. On the bottom half of the bread, arrange the ingredients in this order: half the olive salad, then all the ham, provolone, and salami. Toss the remaining olive salad with the chicken and place on top. Cover with the top of the bread and wrap tightly in aluminum foil. Let rest in the refrigerator for at least 4 or up to 24 hours. Let the muffuletta come to room temperature, cut into 4 wedges, and serve.

CHICKEN & LEMON PANINI

Serves 4

2 whole chicken breasts
    (about 2¼ pounds)

8 fresh flat-leaf parsley sprigs, plus
    2 teaspoons minced fresh
    flat-leaf parsley

2 garlic cloves, halved

½ teaspoon whole black
    peppercorns

6 tablespoons (¾ stick) unsalted
    butter, at room temperature

¾ teaspoon grated lemon zest

1½ teaspoons fresh lemon juice,
    or to taste

Salt & freshly ground pepper

8 slices crusty country-style
    white bread

4 radicchio leaves or watercress
    sprigs (optional)

PANINI ARE SANDWICHES ITALIAN STYLE.
USE THE HIGHEST-QUALITY BREAD YOU CAN FIND.
I USED A SOURDOUGH LOAF ABOUT FIVE
AND A HALF INCHES WIDE AND THREE AND A HALF
HIGH. TRY TO EAT THIS SANDWICH
WHILE IT IS STILL WARM—IT'S PURE BLISS.

In a large deep skillet, put the chicken, parsley sprigs, garlic, peppercorns, and enough cold water to cover. Bring to a boil over high heat. Reduce the heat and simmer for 15 minutes, turning the chicken once if necessary. Remove from the heat and set aside for 20 minutes. Drain the chicken and when cool enough to handle, discard the skin and bones and cut the meat against the grain into thin slices.

In a small bowl, combine the butter, minced parsley, lemon zest, and lemon juice, and season with salt and pepper.

Spread each slice of bread with the lemon butter. Top 4 of the bread slices with the sliced chicken and the radicchio, if using. Top with the remaining bread and gently press down. Cut each panini in half, transfer to serving plates, and serve while still warm.

Serves 4

SOFT TACOS ARE MADE FROM FLOUR
TORTILLAS THAT ARE HEATED, PILED WITH A VARIETY OF
FILLINGS, FOLDED UP, AND EATEN OUT OF HAND.
MY TACOS ARE PATTERNED AFTER THE GREAT SOFT TACOS
I'VE GOTTEN AT TACO STANDS IN EAST L.A.

Put the chicken into a large deep skillet, add cold water to cover, and bring to a boil over high heat. Reduce the heat and simmer for 15 minutes. Remove from the heat and set aside for 20 minutes. Drain and when cool enough to handle, finely shred the meat, discarding the skin and bones.

Combine the chicken, onions, cilantro, chile powder, and the anise seeds, if desired, in a large bowl, and season with salt and hot pepper sauce. Cover to keep warm.

In a small bowl, combine the tomatoes, scallions, and 1½ teaspoons of the lime juice and season with salt and hot pepper sauce. In another small bowl, combine the avocado and the remaining 1½ teaspoons lime juice, and season with salt and hot pepper sauce.

In a medium-size dry skillet, heat the tortillas, one at a time, turning once, over medium heat. Keep warm.

To serve, mound the lettuce in the center of a platter. Place the tomato mixture, avocado mixture, radishes, and lime wedges in separate mounds around the lettuce. If necessary, gently reheat the chicken mixture, and transfer to a serving bowl. Place the warmed tortillas in a basket and serve immediately, letting your guests assemble their own tacos.

2 whole chicken breasts (about 2¼ pounds), split

½ cup minced sweet white onions

⅓ cup packed fresh cilantro leaves

¼ teaspoon ancho chile powder, or to taste

Pinch of anise seeds, lightly crushed (optional)

Salt & hot pepper sauce

2 cups chopped tomatoes

2 scallions, chopped

1 tablespoon fresh lime juice, or to taste

1 ripe California avocado, peeled, pitted & cut into ¼-inch dice

12 corn tortillas

Finely shredded romaine lettuce

4 radishes, halved & thinly sliced

Lime wedges, for garnish

CHICKEN SALAD TEA SANDWICHES

2 whole chicken breasts
  (about 2¼ pounds)

½ cup mayonnaise, plus additional,
  for spreading

⅓ cup minced shallots

1 teaspoon minced fresh tarragon

½ teaspoon grated lemon zest

Salt & freshly ground pepper

24 very thin slices white bread

½ cup finely chopped smoked
  almonds

WHEN I WORKED FOR BESPOKE FOOD,
A CATERING COMPANY IN NEW YORK CITY, WE MADE
THOUSANDS OF THESE SANDWICHES TO
SERVE AS HORS D'OEUVRES, AND THEY WERE THE FAVORITE
AT EVERY PARTY. TO MAKE THE SANDWICHES
AHEAD, LAYER THEM IN A CONTAINER, WRAP TIGHTLY WITH
PLASTIC WRAP, ADD A LAYER OF MOIST PAPER
TOWELS, AND TOP WITH ANOTHER LAYER OF PLASTIC WRAP.

Put the chicken into a large deep skillet, add enough cold water to cover, and bring to a boil over high heat. Reduce the heat and simmer for 15 minutes. Remove from the heat and set aside for 20 minutes. Drain the chicken and when cool enough to handle, finely shred the meat, discarding the skin and bones.

In a medium-size bowl, combine the chicken, mayonnaise, shallots, tarragon, and lemon zest and season with salt and pepper.

Spread the chicken salad on 12 slices of the bread and cover with the remaining 12 slices, pressing down gently to slightly compress the sandwiches.

Using a 2-inch round cutter, cut 2 rounds from each sandwich. Lightly spread the edges of the rounds with mayonnaise, coating evenly.

Put the almonds on a small plate and roll the edge of each sandwich in the almonds. The sandwiches can be made up to 2 hours ahead, wrapped in plastic wrap, and refrigerated.

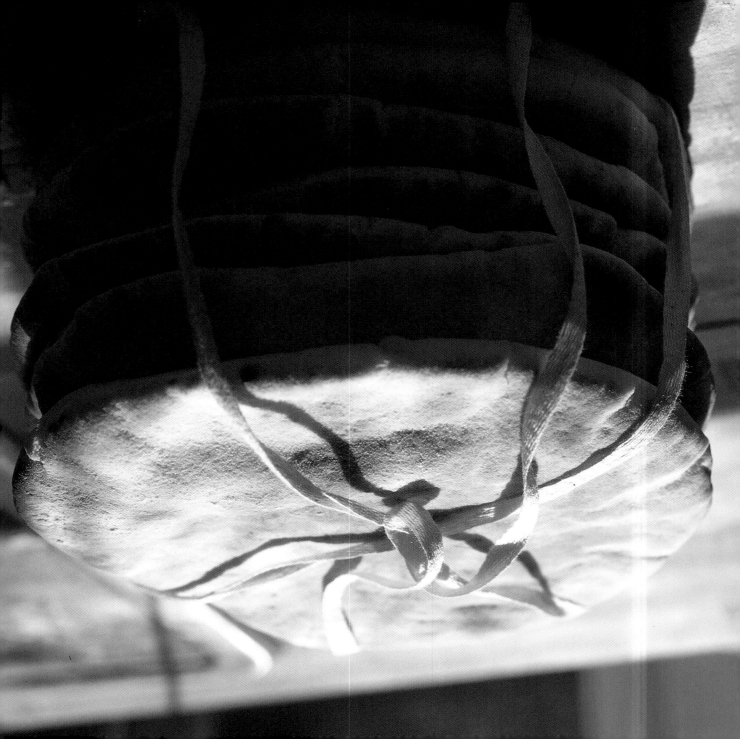

CHICKEN WITH SUMAC & CARDAMOM

Serves 6

I FIRST ENJOYED THIS SANDWICH IN JORDAN, AND I COULDN'T WAIT TO MAKE IT WHEN I RETURNED HOME. THE EXOTIC FRUITY FLAVOR OF THE SUMAC PAIRS PARTICULARLY WELL WITH THE CHICKEN, ONION, AND CARDAMOM.

⅓ cup fruity olive oil

8 small red onions, sliced

3 garlic cloves, thinly sliced lengthwise

8 green cardamom pods, lightly crushed

½ teaspoon ground allspice

Salt & freshly ground pepper

1 (3½-pound) chicken, quartered

¼ cup pine nuts, toasted

2 tablespoons ground sumac*

Six 7-inch soft pita breads, preferably pocketless, warmed

Fresh cilantro leaves, for garnish

*Sumac is available in Middle Eastern food markets and from mail order sources

In a large cast-iron or other heavy skillet, heat the oil over medium heat until hot but not smoking. Add the onions, garlic, 4 of the cardamom pods, and the allspice, and season with salt and pepper. Reduce the heat to low and cook, stirring occasionally, for 1½ hours, or until soft and caramelized. Remove from the heat and discard the cardamom pods.

Meanwhile, put the chicken into a large deep skillet, add enough cold water to cover and the remaining 4 cardamom pods. Bring to a boil over high heat. Reduce the heat and simmer, turning the chicken once if necessary, for 45 minutes, or until cooked through. Remove the chicken to a large plate, and, when cool enough to handle, coarsely shred the meat, discarding the skin and bones.

Stir the chicken, pine nuts, and sumac into the onions, and season with salt and pepper. Place the pitas on a work surface. Place the chicken mixture in the center of the pitas and garnish with the cilantro. To facilitate eating the sandwiches, fold over the sides of the bread and wrap the bottoms with foil. Serve warm.

CHICKEN SOUVLAKI
WITH MINT TZATZIKI

Serves 4

TZATZIKI

1 English cucumber, halved, seeded & cut into ¼-inch dice

Salt

2 cups plain yogurt, drained for at least 2 hours & squeezed dry

2 tablespoons fruity olive oil

2 tablespoons minced fresh mint

1 teaspoon red wine vinegar

1 or 2 garlic cloves, mashed to a paste with ¼ teaspoon salt

Freshly ground pepper

¼ cup each fruity olive oil & red wine vinegar

2 teaspoons each minced fresh oregano & thyme

Salt & freshly ground pepper

4 boneless skinless chicken breast halves, cut into ½-inch-wide diagonal strips

Four 7-inch soft pita breads, preferably pocketless

2 cups finely shredded romaine lettuce

½ small red onion, thinly sliced

1 tomato, cut into 8 wedges

VARIATIONS ON THIS CUCUMBER-YOGURT CONDIMENT ARE POPULAR FROM NORTHERN INDIA THROUGH THE BALKANS AND INTO GREECE. IN TURKEY IT'S CALLED CACIK, IN INDIA IT'S RAITA, AND IN GREECE, IT'S CALLED TZATZIKI.

Prepare the tzatziki: Toss together the cucumber and 1 teaspoon salt in a colander set over a medium-size bowl, and let drain for 1 hour. In a small bowl, combine the yogurt, cucumber, oil, mint, vinegar, and garlic paste, and season with salt and pepper. Let stand at room temperature for 1 hour.

In a small bowl, combine the oil, vinegar, oregano, and thyme, and season with salt and pepper. Add the chicken, turning to coat. Cover and marinate in the refrigerator for at least 2 hours.

Preheat a grill to hot and brush with oil.

Thread the chicken onto four 8- to 10-inch metal skewers. Strain the marinade into a small saucepan and bring to a boil over high heat.

Grill the chicken, basting with the marinade, for 3 to 5 minutes. Turn, baste again, and cook for 3 to 5 minutes longer, or until the chicken is cooked through. Warm the pitas on the grill.

Remove the chicken from the skewers. Place the pitas on a work surface and top with the lettuce, chicken, onion, tomato, and some tzatziki. Fold over the sides of the bread and wrap the bottom with foil. (If using pita bread with pockets, cut a small slice off of one side and fill with the lettuce, chicken, onion, tomatoes, and tzatziki.) Serve warm.

COLD SESAME NOODLES WITH CHICKEN

Serves 6

HOW MANY TIMES HAVE YOU HAD
SESAME NOODLES IN A RESTAURANT AND WISHED THAT
YOU COULD MAKE THEM YOURSELF—AND THAT
YOU COULD HAVE THEM AS AN ENTREE RATHER THAN
JUST AN APPETIZER? YOU CAN.

¼ cup each soy sauce, Asian sesame oil & creamy natural peanut butter

3 tablespoons chicken broth, brewed black tea, or water

2 tablespoons rice or distilled white vinegar, or to taste

1 tablespoon packed dark brown sugar

1 or 2 garlic cloves, minced

1 teaspoon minced peeled fresh ginger

1 pound thin spaghetti

Salt & ground red pepper

6 boneless skinless chicken breast halves (about 5 ounces each)

3 tablespoons canola or other vegetable oil

2 scallions, cut into thin diagonal slices

3 tablespoons minced fresh cilantro

1½ cups thinly sliced seeded English cucumber

1 carrot, cut into long thin shreds

In a large bowl, whisk together the soy sauce, 3½ tablespoons of the sesame oil, the peanut butter, broth, vinegar, brown sugar, garlic, and ginger until well combined. Set aside.

Cook the spaghetti in a large pot of boiling salted water according to the package directions, until al dente. Drain in a colander and immediately toss the noodles with the sesame oil mixture. Season with salt and ground red pepper. Let cool to room temperature, then cover, and refrigerate for 1 hour, or until cold.

Preheat a grill to hot and brush with oil or preheat a grill pan.

On a large plate, drizzle the chicken with the canola oil, turning to coat. Season with salt and ground red pepper. Grill the chicken for 5 to 7 minutes on each side, or until cooked through. Remove to a cutting board and when cool enough to handle, cut into thin diagonal slices.

In a large bowl, combine the chicken, the remaining 1½ teaspoons sesame oil, the scallions, and 2 tablespoons of the cilantro.

To serve, arrange the noodles on a serving platter, placing the cucumber and carrot around them, then top with the chicken, and sprinkle with the remaining 1 tablespoon cilantro.

RED-COOKED
CHICKEN WINGS

Serves 8

16 chicken wings, wing tips cut off
& discarded, separated at the
second joint

1 cup cold water

½ cup each soy sauce & dry sherry

¼ cup packed dark brown sugar

3 strips orange zest (removed
with a vegetable peeler)

4 garlic cloves, crushed

1 teaspoon Asian sesame oil

2 star anise

½ teaspoon Chinese five-spice
powder

Ground red pepper

4 scallions, cut into 1-inch lengths,
plus minced scallions,
for garnish

Fresh cilantro leaves, for garnish

THIS IS ONE OF THE FIRST DISHES I EVER COOKED. (I THINK IT CAME RIGHT AFTER CHOCOLATE CHIP COOKIES AND BROWNIES.) I SAW A RECIPE SOMEWHERE, AND JUST HAD TO MAKE IT. I HAVE SINCE ADDED THE STAR ANISE, THE FIVE-SPICE POWDER, AND THE FRESH CILANTRO LEAVES, NONE OF WHICH I'D EVEN HEARD OF WHEN I FIRST BEGAN COOKING. I LOVE TO TAKE THESE WINGS ON PICNICS AND NIBBLE ON THEM WITH DRINKS.

In a Dutch oven, combine the wings, water, soy sauce, sherry, brown sugar, orange zest, garlic, sesame oil, star anise, five-spice powder, and ground red pepper to taste. Cover and bring to a boil over high heat. Reduce the heat and simmer for 20 minutes, stirring occasionally.

Stir in the scallions and simmer, uncovered, stirring occasionally, for about 15 minutes longer, or until the chicken is cooked through. Let the chicken cool to room temperature in the broth, then refrigerate, covered, until ready to serve.

To serve, remove the wings from the liquid, arrange on a platter, and sprinkle with the minced scallions and cilantro.

26   SUMMER

THAI-STYLE CHICKEN SATÉ

CURRY PASTE MARINADE

¼ cup well-stirred unsweetened
    coconut milk

1 tablespoon Thai Green Curry
    Paste (recipe follows)

3 boneless skinless chicken breast
    halves (about 5 ounces each),
    each cut diagonally into 6 strips

CUCUMBER SALAD

1 cup rice vinegar

¾ cup sugar

1 large English cucumber, halved
    lengthwise & thinly sliced

4 large shallots, thinly sliced

¼ cup fresh cilantro leaves

1 to 2 tablespoons minced, seeded
    fresh red & green Thai chiles
    or other hot chiles

1 teaspoon salt

PEANUT SAUCE

1 tablespoon canola or other
    vegetable oil

1 small shallot, minced

¼ cup well-stirred unsweetened
    coconut milk

THAI COOKS USE WONDERFUL, INTENSELY
FLAVORED CURRY PASTES THAT THEY MAKE AT HOME OR
PURCHASE IN THE MARKET. YOU CAN BUY
THESE INEXPENSIVE PRODUCTS (THE BEST COME IN PLASTIC
TUBS) IN ASIAN MARKETS OR MAKE YOUR
OWN. THE BEST CURRY PASTES FOR THIS RECIPE ARE THE
CLASSIC RED, GREEN, OR YELLOW. TRY
ALL THREE TO SEE WHICH IS YOUR OWN PERSONAL FAVORITE.

Soak eighteen 7-inch bamboo skewers in water to cover for at least 30 minutes.

Prepare the curry paste marinade: In a medium-size bowl, stir together the coconut milk and curry paste until well combined. Add the chicken and turn to coat. Cover and marinate in the refrigerator for about 1 hour, turning occasionally.

Preheat a grill to high and brush with oil.

Prepare the cucumber salad: In a medium bowl, stir together the vinegar and sugar until the sugar has dissolved. Stir in the remaining ingredients and set aside at room temperature, stirring occasionally.

Prepare the peanut sauce: Heat the oil in a small heavy skillet over medium heat until hot but not smoking. Add the shallot and cook, stirring, for about 4 minutes, or until lightly browned. Add the coconut milk, broth, peanut butter, and brown sugar, and season with salt. Bring just to a boil. Reduce the heat to low and cook, stirring, for 1 to 2 minutes, or just until the sauce is thick and smooth. Remove from the heat. (The sauces will thicken on standing; thin to the desired consistency if necessary with a bit of broth or water.)

Thread the chicken onto the skewers; discard the marinade. Grill or broil for 2 to 3 minutes. Turn and grill or broil for 2 to 3 minutes longer, or until the chicken is golden and just cooked through.

To serve, arrange the saté on a platter. Transfer the peanut sauce to a small serving bowl and put the cucumber salad on a small plate.

¼ cup chicken broth, plus additional to thin the sauce if necessary

2 tablespoons creamy natural peanut butter

1 teaspoon packed dark brown sugar

Salt

THAI GREEN CURRY PASTE

Makes about ³/₄ cup

In a large mortar and pestle, pound the coriander seeds, cumin seeds, and peppercorns to a powder. Gradually add the shallots, chiles, lemon grass, and garlic, and pound until smooth. Add the cilantro and pound until a smooth paste has formed. (Alternatively, this may be done in a food processor, adding a bit of water.) Transfer the curry paste to a bowl and add the shrimp paste and season with salt, stirring until smooth. The curry paste may be stored, refrigerated, in an air-tight container for a few weeks.

2 tablespoons each coriander & cumin seeds

1 teaspoon whole black peppercorns

2 shallots, chopped

5 tiny Thai chiles, seeded & chopped

2 stalks lemon grass, chopped (tender inner part only)

3 garlic cloves, chopped

¼ cup plus 2 tablespoons chopped fresh cilantro

1 teaspoon shrimp paste

Salt

CHICKEN SAUTE WITH PEACHES & BASIL

Serves 4

2 small ripe peaches

¼ cup all-purpose flour

Salt & freshly ground pepper

4 boneless skinless chicken
  breast halves (about
  5 ounces each)

2 tablespoons unsalted butter

¾ cup chicken broth

2 shallots, minced

¼ teaspoon grated lemon zest

3 fresh basil leaves, finely shredded,
  plus tiny whole sprigs,
  for garnish

PEACHES AND BASIL HAVE ALWAYS
BEEN ONE OF MY FAVORITE FLAVOR COMBINATIONS:
EVEN MORE THAN TOMATOES AND
BASIL. THEY REMIND ME OF ALL THE BEST
THINGS ABOUT SUMMERTIME.

Plunge the peaches into a large saucepan of boiling water for 1 minute. Remove and set aside.

On a plate, combine the flour, ½ teaspoon salt, and ½ teaspoon pepper. Lightly coat the chicken breasts with the seasoned flour, shaking off the excess.

In a large cast-iron or other heavy skillet, melt the butter over medium heat. Add the chicken and cook, turning once, for 10 to 12 minutes, or until cooked through. Remove to a plate and cover to keep warm.

Peel, halve, and pit the peaches and cut into ½-inch-thick wedges.

Pour the broth into the skillet and increase the heat to high. Deglaze the skillet by bringing the broth to a boil and scraping to loosen any browned bits in the bottom of the pan. Add the peaches, shallots, and lemon zest. Cook, stirring frequently, for about 3 minutes, or until the sauce has thickened. Stir in the shredded basil and season with salt and pepper.

To serve, place the chicken on serving plates, spoon the sauce over, and garnish with the tiny basil sprigs.

GRILLED CHICKEN QUESADILLAS

TOMATILLO SALSA

¼ cup coarsely chopped sweet white onion

1 pound fresh tomatillos (10 medium to large), papery skin removed, washed & quartered

¼ cup chopped fresh cilantro

1 jalapeño chile, seeded & chopped

1 tablespoon olive oil

1 garlic clove, minced

1 teaspoon sugar

Salt & hot pepper sauce

3 boneless skinless chicken breast halves (about 5 ounces each)

1 tablespoon olive oil

Salt & hot pepper sauce

8 (7-inch) flour tortillas

2 cups grated queso fresco blanco, Monterey Jack, or Monterey Jack with habanero chiles or jalapeños

2 poblano chiles, roasted, peeled, cored, seeded & chopped

THESE QUESADILLAS ARE GREAT SERVED WITH A BIG SALAD OF ROMAINE AND SLICED ORANGES, OR IF YOU'D RATHER, RICE AND BEANS.

Preheat the grill to medium and brush with oil.

Prepare the tomatillo salsa: In a food processor, pulse the onion until finely chopped. Add the tomatillos, cilantro, jalapeño, oil, garlic, sugar, salt, and hot pepper sauce to taste, pulsing until the tomatillos are coarsely chopped. Transfer to a medium-size bowl.

On a large plate, drizzle the chicken with the oil, turning to coat. Season with salt and hot pepper sauce. Grill the chicken, turning once, for 5 to 7 minutes on each side, or until cooked through. When cool enough to handle, cut into thin diagonal slices.

Meanwhile, drain the tomatillo salsa in a fine-mesh strainer set over a bowl for 10 minutes.

Preheat the oven to 450°F.

In a large bowl, combine the chicken and tomatillo salsa.

In a dry skillet over medium-high heat, heat the tortillas, one at a time, turning once, until puffed and brown.

Combine the cheese and poblanos in a medium-size bowl. Sprinkle over the tortillas, leaving a ½-inch border all around. Divide the chicken mixture among the tortillas. Fold the tortillas in half, place on 1 or 2 baking sheets, and bake for about 10 minutes, or until the cheese is melted and the tortillas begin to crisp. Serve hot.

CHICKEN WITH CHERRIES & THYME

Serves 4

I LOVE THE AFFECT THE FLAVOR OF FRESH THYME
HAS ON FRUITS. HERE, THE RICH SWEETNESS OF RIPE BING
CHERRIES BECOMES HEIGHTENED WHEN COMBINED
WITH THE COOL HERBAL TASTE OF THYME. MAKE THIS
WHEN CHERRIES ARE AT THEIR PEAK, AND SEE IF
YOU LIKE IT BEST WITH BING OR THE MORE DELICATELY
FLAVORED QUEEN ANN CHERRIES.

¼ cup all-purpose flour

Salt & freshly ground pepper

4 boneless skinless chicken breast
halves (about 5 ounces each)

2 tablespoons unsalted butter

¾ cup chicken broth

1 teaspoon fresh lime juice,
or to taste

1 small red onion, thinly sliced

¾ cup ripe Bing or Queen Anne
cherries, stemmed & pitted

½ teaspoon fresh thyme leaves, plus
whole sprigs, for garnish

Pinch of grated lime zest

On a large plate, combine the flour, ½ teaspoon salt, and ½ teaspoon pepper. Lightly coat the chicken breasts with the seasoned flour, shaking off the excess flour.

In a large cast-iron or other heavy skillet, melt the butter over medium heat. Add the chicken and cook, turning once, for 10 to 12 minutes, or until cooked through. Remove to a plate and cover to keep warm.

Pour the broth and lime juice into the skillet and increase the heat to medium-high. Deglaze the skillet by bringing the liquid to a boil and scraping to loosen any browned bits in bottom of the pan. Add the onion, cherries, thyme, and lime zest. Cook, stirring frequently, for 3 minutes, or until the sauce has thickened. Season with salt and pepper.

To serve, place the chicken breasts on serving plates, spoon the sauce over, and garnish with the thyme sprigs.

CHICKEN & RADISH STIR-FRY

Serves 4

NOT AT ALL TRADITIONALLY CHINESE, THIS
IS AN UNUSUALLY FLAVORFUL AND ATTRACTIVE DISH. IT
OFFERS THE SWEETNESS OF HOISIN SAUCE, THE
HEAT OF GROUND RED PEPPER, A WONDERFUL SLIGHTLY
BITTER FLAVOR FROM THE WATERCRESS, AND
THE PUNGENT TASTE OF RADISHES. IT'S ALSO QUICK AND
EASY, WITHOUT THE USUAL THIRTY MINUTES
OF CHOPPING OFTEN REQUIRED FOR STIR-FRYING. JUST
MINCE THE SCALLIONS AND SLICE THE CUCUMBER
AND RADISHES AND YOU'RE THERE—IN LESS THAN TEN
MINUTES OF COOKING YOU'VE GOT DINNER.

3 tablespoons canola or other vegetable oil

4 boneless skinless chicken breast halves (about 5 ounces each), cut into ½-inch-wide diagonal strips

Salt & ground red pepper

4 small scallions, minced

2 tablespoons hoisin sauce

1 bunch watercress, tough stems discarded

½ English cucumber, halved, seeded & cut into thin diagonal slices

4 radishes, halved & thinly sliced

1 teaspoon sesame seeds, toasted, for garnish (optional)

Hot cooked rice, for serving

In a well-seasoned wok or a large heavy skillet, heat 2 tablespoons of the oil over medium-high heat until hot but not smoking. Add the chicken, season with salt and ground red pepper, and stir-fry for about 4 minutes, or until the chicken is just cooked thorough. Stir in half of the scallions and the hoisin sauce, transfer to a bowl, and cover to keep warm.

Wipe out the wok, add the remaining 1 tablespoon oil, and heat until hot but not smoking. Add the watercress, cucumber, and radishes, and season with salt and ground red pepper. Stir-fry about for 2 minutes, or just until the vegetables are wilted and heated through.

To serve, place the chicken on a serving platter, top with the watercress mixture, and garnish with remaining scallions and the sesame seeds, if desired. Serve with the hot rice.

JERK CHICKEN WINGS

5 pounds chicken wings, wing
    tips cut off & discarded,
    separated at the second joint

10 scallions, chopped

1 to 3 Scotch bonnet or jalapeño
    chiles, seeded & chopped

4 bay leaves, broken in half

2 tablespoons distilled white vinegar

4 garlic cloves, thinly sliced

1 tablespoon ground allspice

2½ teaspoons dried thyme

1¼ teaspoons salt

½ teaspoon ground red pepper

½ teaspoon freshly ground black
    pepper

SCOTCH BONNETS ARE THE CHILES USED IN JAMAICA FOR JERK SAUCE. THEY ARE VERY HOT AND NOT ALWAYS EASY TO FIND. IF YOU WOULD RATHER, USE AN EQUAL AMOUNT (OR MORE) OF JALAPEÑOS. JERK CHICKEN IS A VERY FORGIVING DISH. THE BEST JERK CHICKEN I'VE EVER HAD WAS AT A ROADSIDE PLACE IN OCHO RIOS, JAMAICA. IT WAS COOKED OUTDOORS OVER AN OPEN FIRE AND OLD CAR FENDERS WERE LAID OVER THE CHICKEN AS A COVER.

Put the chicken wings into a large bowl and set aside.

In a food processor or blender, combine all the remaining ingredients and process until smooth and thick. Spoon over the chicken, turning until well coated. Cover and refrigerate overnight, turning occasionally.

Preheat the broiler.

Place half the wings on the broiler pan and broil, 4 to 5 inches from the heat, for about 10 minutes on each side—the wings should be dark brown but not burned. Transfer to a serving platter. Scrape the charred marinade from the broiler pan and spread on the wings, if desired. Repeat with remaining chicken wings. Serve at room temperature.

CHICKEN WITH CORN & AVOCADO SALSA

Serves 4

THIS SIMPLE GRILLED CHICKEN DISH HAS ALL THE BEST FLAVORS OF SUMMER—CORN, TOMATOES, AND BASIL. GETTING THE FRESHEST, BEST PRODUCE YOU CAN FIND WILL MAKE ALL THE DIFFERENCE HERE: THIS IS DEFINITELY NOT A RECIPE TO MAKE IN JANUARY.

Preheat the grill to hot and brush with oil.

Prepare the corn and avocado salsa: In a medium-size bowl, combine the corn, cherry tomatoes, avocado, onion, basil, 1 tablespoon of the oil, the lime juice, and garlic, and season with salt and pepper. Set aside.

On a large plate, drizzle the chicken with the oil, turning to coat. Season with salt and pepper.

Grill the chicken, for 5 to 7 minutes each side, or until cooked through.

To serve, place the chicken on serving plates, top with the corn and avocado salsa, and sprinkle with the basil.

CORN & AVOCADO SALSA

1 ear fresh corn, kernels removed

8 small cherry tomatoes, quartered

½ ripe California avocado, peeled, pitted & finely chopped

2 tablespoons finely chopped red onion

2 fresh basil leaves, shredded

1 tablespoon canola or other vegetable oil

2 teaspoons fresh lime juice, or to taste

1 small garlic clove, minced

Salt & freshly ground pepper

4 boneless skinless chicken breast halves (about 5 ounces each)

2 tablespoons canola or other vegetable oil

Salt & freshly ground pepper

2 fresh basil leaves, shredded, for garnish

CHICKEN TANDOORI WITH GRILLED ONIONS

Serves 4

1 cup plain yogurt

1 small onion, minced

3 tablespoons canola or other vegetable oil

2 tablespoons fresh lemon juice

1½ tablespoons grated peeled fresh ginger

1 tablespoon garam masala

2 garlic cloves, minced

Salt & ground red pepper

1 (3- to 3½-pound) chicken, cut into quarters & wing tips discarded

2 medium-size Vidalia, Texas Sweet or other onions, halved

1 tablespoon minced fresh cilantro, plus whole sprigs, for garnish

Lemon wedges, for garnish

IN THE PUNJAB WHERE TANDOORI ORIGINATED, CHICKEN IS MARINATED IN A SPICY MIXTURE AND THEN ROASTED IN A CYLINDRICAL OVEN CALLED A TANDOOR. IT IS ABOUT FOUR FEET HIGH, CONSTRUCTED OF STRAW AND MUD, AND PARTIALLY SUNK INTO THE GROUND. SINCE TANDOOR OVENS ARE NOT COMMON IN THIS COUNTRY, THIS RECIPE HAS BEEN ADAPTED TO A CHARCOAL FIRE.

In a baking dish just large enough to hold the chicken in a single layer, whisk together the yogurt, minced onion, 2 tablespoons of the oil, the lemon juice, ginger, garam masala, and garlic, and season with salt and ground red pepper. Add the chicken and turn to coat. Cover and marinate in the refrigerator for at least 3 or up to 24 hours, turning occasionally.

Preheat a grill to hot and brush with oil.

Grill the chicken, skin side down, basting occasionally with the reserved marinade, for 12 to 15 minutes. Turn, baste again, and cook for 10 to 12 minutes longer, or until the skin is browned and the chicken is cooked through. Meanwhile, brush the onions with the remaining 1 tablespoon oil and grill alongside the chicken, turning it, for about 20 minutes, or until softened; transfer to a plate and cover to keep warm.

To serve, arrange the chicken and onions on a serving platter, sprinkle with the minced cilantro, and garnish with the cilantro sprigs and lemon wedges.

LIME & GINGER GRILLED CHICKEN

Serves 4

THE COMBINATION OF LIME JUICE,
RUM, GINGER, THYME, AND ALLSPICE IS UNIQUELY CARIBBEAN,
AND PERFECT FOR A BACKYARD BARBECUE.

½ cup soy sauce

½ cup each fresh lime juice
& dark rum

1 jalapeño chile, seeded & minced

1 tablespoon minced peeled
fresh ginger

2 garlic cloves, smashed

1 teaspoon fresh thyme leaves

½ teaspoon ground allspice

½ teaspoon freshly ground pepper

8 chicken thighs (about 2 pounds)

Lime wedges, for garnish

In a large bowl, whisk together the soy sauce, lime juice, rum, jalapeño, ginger, garlic, thyme, allspice, and pepper. Add the chicken and turn to coat. Cover and marinate in the refrigerator for at least 3 hours, turning occasionally.

Preheat the grill to hot and brush with oil or preheat the broiler.

Strain the marinade into a small saucepan and bring to a boil. Remove from the heat.

Grill or broil the chicken, skin side down, 5 to 6 inches from the heat, for about 10 minutes, basting occasionally with the reserved marinade. Turn, baste again, and cook for 8 to 10 minutes longer, or until the skin is browned and the juices run clear when pierced with a paring knife.

To serve, place the chicken on a platter and garnish with the lime wedges.

ALL-AMERICAN BARBECUED CHICKEN

Serves 8

BARBECUE SAUCE

3 tablespoons butter or vegetable oil

1 small onion, finely chopped

1 garlic clove, minced

1 cup cold water

1 cup ketchup

1 small red bell pepper, halved, cored, seeded & finely chopped

½ cup finely chopped celery, including some leaves

3 tablespoons packed brown sugar

2 tablespoons apple cider vinegar

1 tablespoon soy sauce

1 teaspoon Worcestershire sauce

1 teaspoon Dijon mustard

Salt & freshly ground pepper

¼ cup fresh lemon juice, or to taste

2 (3- to 3 ½-pound) chickens, each cut into 8 pieces

THIS SAUCE IS ADAPTED FROM ONE IN THE JOY OF COOKING. IT'S THE FIRST I EVER MADE AND THE ONE MOST AMERICANS GREW UP ON. USE AN EQUIVALENT WEIGHT OF CHICKEN BREASTS, WHOLE LEGS, THIGHS, OR GAME HENS, IF YOU PREFER.

Prepare the barbecue sauce: In a medium-size saucepan, melt the butter over medium heat. Add the onion and garlic and cook, stirring, for 7 minutes, or just until the onion begins to brown. Stir in the water, ketchup, bell pepper, celery, brown sugar, vinegar, soy sauce, Worcestershire sauce, and mustard, and season with salt and pepper. Bring to a boil, then reduce the heat and simmer, stirring occasionally, for 30 minutes. Stir in the lemon juice and remove from the heat.

Preheat the grill to hot and brush with oil or preheat the broiler.

Grill or broil the chicken, 5 to 6 inches from the heat, skin side down, for about 5 minutes. Baste with the barbecue sauce and cook for 5 minutes. Turn, baste again, and cook for 4 to 5 minutes longer, or until the juices from the thigh run clear when pierced with a paring knife and the skin is browned but not burned. Remove the chicken from the heat and brush with more sauce, if desired. Serve hot or at room temperature.

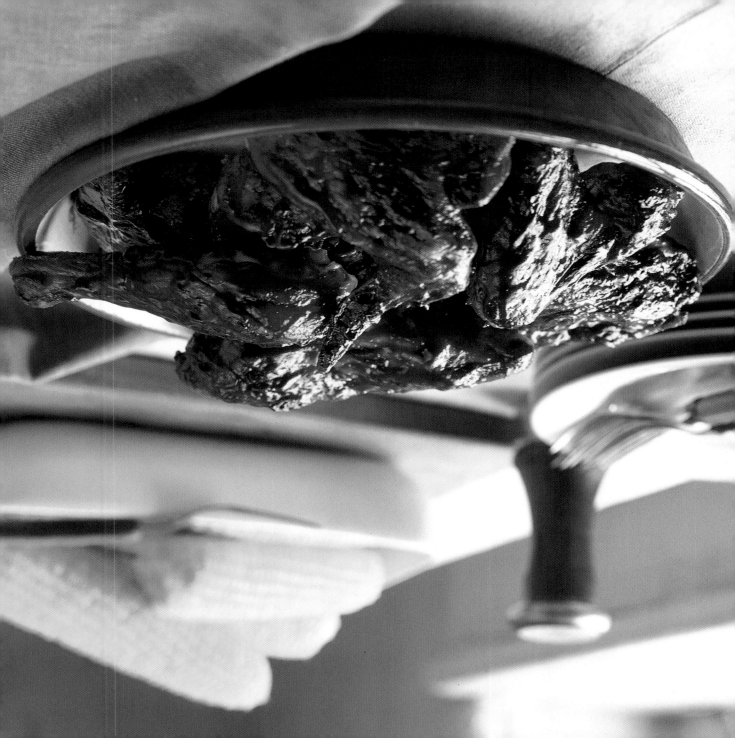

TEQUILA-LIME
GRILLED CHICKEN

TEQUILA-LIME MARINADE

½ cup fresh lime juice

¼ cup tequila

3 tablespoons canola or other vegetable oil

2 tablespoons Triple Sec

4 sprigs fresh cilantro

1 jalapeño chile, seeded & minced

1 garlic clove, halved

1 teaspoon ground coriander

Salt

1 (3- to 3½-pound) chicken, cut into 8 pieces

2 teaspoons minced cilantro, for garnish

THIS MARGARITA-FLAVORED CHICKEN IS PERFECT ON A HOT SUMMER DAY. WHETHER OR NOT YOU SERVE IT WITH MARGARITAS IS UP TO YOU.

Prepare the tequila-lime marinade: In a large bowl, combine the lime juice, tequila, oil, Triple Sec, cilantro, jalapeño, garlic, coriander, and salt to taste. Add the chicken and turn to coat. Cover and marinate in the refrigerator for at least 2 or up to 8 hours, turning occasionally.

Preheat the grill to hot and brush with oil or preheat the broiler.

Transfer the chicken to a plate and pour the marinade through a strainer into a small saucepan and bring to a boil over high heat. Remove from the heat.

Grill or broil the chicken, 5 to 6 inches from the heat, skin side down, for about 10 minutes, basting occasionally with the marinade. Turn the chicken, and cook for 10 to 15 minutes longer, basting frequently, or until the skin is nicely browned and the chicken is cooked through.

Place the chicken on a platter and sprinkle with the cilantro. Serve warm or at room temperature.

GAME HENS WITH BASIL & ORANGE

ORANGES AREN'T REALLY A SUMMER
FRUIT, BUT WHEN COMBINED WITH BASIL, THEY
SEEM VERY SUMMERY. THE CINNAMON
ADDS A THIRD DIMENSION AND ALL THREE COMPLEMENT
EACH OTHER BEAUTIFULLY.

3 small garlic cloves

Salt

Zest of 1 navel orange, removed in strips with a vegetable peeler, plus ¼ teaspoon grated orange zest

1 cup fresh orange juice

3 tablespoons fruity olive oil

2 tablespoons fresh lemon juice

¼ cup finely shredded fresh basil, plus 2 whole leaves

1-inch piece cinnamon stick, broken in half

Ground red pepper

2 Cornish game hens (about 1½ pounds each), backbones removed & halved lengthwise

In a mortar and pestle, mash 2 of the garlic cloves to a paste with ¼ teaspoon salt.

In a shallow baking dish just large enough to hold the game hens laid out flat, stir together the garlic mixture, strips of orange zest, orange juice, oil, lemon juice, shredded basil, cinnamon stick, and ground red pepper. Add the game hens and turn to coat. Cover and marinate in the refrigerator for at least 2 hours, turning occasionally.

Preheat the grill and brush with oil.

Pour the marinade through a strainer into a small saucepan and bring to a boil. Remove from the heat.

Grill the game hens, skin side down, for about 10 minutes, basting occasionally with the reserved marinade. Turn, baste again, and cook for 8 to 10 minutes longer, or until the skin is browned and the juices from the thigh run clear when pierced with a paring knife.

Meanwhile, mince together the remaining garlic clove, basil leaves, and grated orange zest.

Transfer the hens to a serving platter, sprinkle with the basil mixture, and serve.

GRILLED CHICKEN WITH CUCUMBER SALSA

Serves 4

THE TROPICAL FLAVOR AND THE GREAT
TEXTURES OF THIS CHILLED CUCUMBER SALSA ARE A
PERFECT FOIL FOR LUSCIOUS HOT GRILLED
CHICKEN BREASTS. THE SALSA CAN BE MADE SEVERAL HOURS
AHEAD AND SET ASIDE IN THE REFRIGERATOR.

CUCUMBER SALSA

½ English cucumber, halved, seeded & thinly sliced

1 firm but ripe mango, peeled, pitted & finely diced

1 scallion, minced

1 tablespoon finely chopped fresh cilantro,

1 tablespoon rice vinegar, or to taste

1 tablespoon canola or other vegetable oil

Salt & ground red pepper

4 boneless skinless chicken breast halves (about 5 ounces each)

2 tablespoons canola or other vegetable oil

Salt & pepper

Cilantro sprigs, for garnish

Prepare the cucumber salsa: In a medium-size bowl, combine the cucumber, mango, scallion, cilantro, vinegar, and oil, and season with salt and ground red pepper. Refrigerate, covered, until ready to serve.

Preheat a grill to hot and brush with oil or preheat the broiler.

On a large plate, drizzle the chicken with the oil, turning to coat. Season with salt and ground red pepper.

Grill or broil the chicken, 5 to 6 inches from the heat, for 5 to 7 minutes on each side, or until cooked through.

To serve, transfer the chicken to serving plates, top with the salsa, and garnish with the cilantro sprigs.

TERIYAKI CHICKEN WITH EGGPLANT

Serves 4

¼ cup plus 2 tablespoons soy sauce

¼ cup mirin (sweet rice wine)

2 tablespoons packed light brown sugar

1 teaspoon minced peeled fresh ginger

1 garlic clove, halved

1 teaspoon Asian sesame oil

8 chicken thighs (about 2 pounds)

2 small Italian eggplants, cut into ¼-inch-thick slices

TERIYAKI, "SHINING BROIL," IS ONE OF THE GLORIES OF JAPANESE CUISINE. DEFINED AS A BROILING METHOD USING A MIRIN-AND-SOY-SAUCE MARINADE, IT IS ONE OF THE BEST-KNOWN JAPANESE DISHES BECAUSE OF ITS APPEALING DELICATE, SWEET FLAVOR. USING THE BROILER IS THE TRADITIONAL COOKING METHOD, BUT IT'S ALSO WONDERFUL COOKED ON THE GRILL.

In a small saucepan, combine the soy sauce, mirin, brown sugar, ginger, garlic, and sesame oil and bring to a simmer over medium heat. Cook, stirring, for about 5 minutes, or until slightly thickened. Strain and let cool.

Place the chicken in a shallow dish just large enough to hold it in a single layer. Pour the marinade over. Cover and marinate in the refrigerator for 1 hour, turning occasionally.

Preheat the grill to hot and brush with oil or preheat the broiler.

Pour the marinade into a small saucepan and bring to a boil.

Grill or broil the eggplant, 5 to 6 inches from the heat, for about 6 minutes. Turn the eggplant, brush generously with the reserved marinade, and cook for about 6 minutes longer, or until soft and tender. Remove to a platter. Meanwhile, grill or broil the chicken, skin side down, for 8 minutes. Turn, brush generously with the marinade, and cook for about 6 minutes longer, brushing occasionally with the marinade. Transfer the chicken and eggplant to a platter and serve hot or at room temperature.

CHICKEN & BAY LEAF KEBABS

Serves 4

1/4 cup thinly sliced red onion

2 garlic cloves, cut into thin slices

14 large bay leaves

1/2 teaspoon minced fresh oregano

1/2 teaspoon hot or sweet paprika

3 tablespoons fruity olive oil

3 tablespoons fresh lemon juice

Salt & freshly ground pepper

4 boneless skinless chicken breast
halves (about 5 ounces each),
each cut into 12 chunks

12 thin lemon slices, seeded
& halved

Hot cooked rice pilaf, for serving

1 tablespoon minced fresh flat-leaf
parsley, for garnish

GRILLED CHICKEN FLAVORED WITH
LEMON AND BAY LEAVES IS ABOUT AS GOOD AS IT GETS.
THE STRONG MEDITERRANEAN FLAVORS MIXED
WITH SMOKE FROM THE GRILL MAKE FOR A PERFECTLY
SIMPLE, PERFECTLY DELICIOUS DISH.

In a large bowl, combine the onion, garlic, 2 of the bay leaves, the oregano, paprika, oil, and lemon juice, and season with salt and pepper. Add the chicken and stir to coat. Marinate in the refrigerator for 1 hour.

Soak the remaining 12 bay leaves and twelve 7-inch bamboo skewers in water to cover for 1 hour. Cut each bay leaf crosswise in half.

Preheat a grill to hot and brush with oil or preheat the broiler.

Remove the chicken from the marinade, reserving the marinade, and thread onto the skewers along with the halved bay leaves and the lemon slices in this order: bay leaf, chicken, lemon slice, chicken, repeating once and placing the ingredients close together. In a small saucepan, bring the reserved marinade to a boil over high heat.

Grill or broil the kebabs, 5 to 6 inches from the heat, for 3 to 5 minutes, basting occasionally with the marinade. Turn the kebabs, baste again, and cook for 2 to 5 minutes longer, or until the chicken is golden and just cooked through.

To serve, divide the rice among serving plates and slide the chicken off the skewers onto the rice. Drizzle the chicken and rice with the warm marinade and sprinkle with the parsley.

GRILLED CHICKEN WITH NECTARINE SALSA

Serves 4

NECTARINE SALSA

1 large ripe nectarine, halved, pitted & cut into ½-inch pieces

½ cup thinly sliced seeded English cucumber

1 small scallion, minced

1 teaspoon fresh lemon juice, or to taste

¼ teaspoon fresh thyme leaves,

Salt & freshly ground pepper

1 tablespoon crumbled feta cheese

4 boneless skinless chicken breast halves (about 5 ounces each)

Salt & pepper

1 tablespoon olive oil

Whole thyme sprigs, for garnish

Preheat a grill to hot and brush with oil or preheat the broiler.

Prepare the nectarine salsa: In a medium-size bowl, combine the nectarine, cucumber, scallion, lemon juice, thyme, and salt and pepper to taste. Set aside at room temperature.

Season the chicken with salt and pepper and brush on both sides with the oil. Grill or broil the chicken, 5 to 6 inches from the heat, for 5 to 7 minutes on each side, or until just cooked through.

To serve, stir the feta into the nectarine mixture. Place the chicken on serving plates, top with the salsa, and garnish with the thyme sprigs.

CHICKEN BASICS

The color of chicken skin is no indication of quality or flavor. Chickens that are yellow are fed marigold petals or more yellow corn than white-skinned chickens.

The texture and flavor of a fresh chicken is superior to a frozen chicken.

Generally count on one or two meaty pieces of chicken per person. Each pound of whole chicken will yield about one cup cooked chicken. Twelve ounces of skinned and boned breasts will yield two cups cooked meat.

PREPARATION SAFETY

Since chicken may carry bacteria that cause food poisoning, it is a good idea to follow a few simple rules when storing, preparing, and cooking chicken.

Chicken is highly perishable so it is best used within two days of the sell-by date on the package.

After buying chicken, get it home and into the refrigerator as quickly as possible—within one hour. Store it in the coldest part of the refrigerator.

When freezing chicken, wrap it tightly in freezer paper, heavy-duty foil, or freezer-weight plastic bags—remember to label and date the package.

Use frozen chicken parts within three months and whole chicken within six. Thaw chicken in the refrigerator or in cold water. Once defrosted, chicken should never be refrozen.

Keep cutting boards, knives, countertops, and hands scrupulously clean by washing with hot soapy water.

COOKING SAFETY

If you have marinated chicken, and intend to brush it with the marinade while grilling, boil the marinade for at least half a minute.

A chicken should be stuffed just before going into the oven. Prepare the stuffing ahead of time and refrigerate it separately. Always loosely stuff poultry, filling it only three quarters full.

The United States Department of Agriculture recommends cooking whole chicken to an internal temperature of 180°F, bone-in parts to 170°F, and boneless chicken breasts to 160°F. We prefer to cook whole chicken, legs, thighs, and drumsticks to 170°F, bone-in breasts to 155°F, and boneless breasts to 150°F. Always err on the side of safety: if you are not sure that the chicken is done, cook it a little longer. Use an instant read thermometer or pierce with a paring knife to see if the juices run clear, with no hint of pink. Salmonella is destroyed at 140°F.

BROILER/FRYER This all-purpose tender young chicken is about 7 weeks old and weighs from two to four pounds. Broilers can be cooked in any manner and can be purchased whole, in split halves, cut into quarters, or by type of part.

FREE-RANGE There must be documented proof showing that these chickens do not consume antibiotics or growth enhancers, and that the chickens have access to a yard. They are more expensive because their care is more labor intensive.

KOSHER These chickens are raised and slaughtered in compliance with Jewish dietary laws. After slaughter, they are salted to draw out the blood. Because of this process, some consider kosher chickens to be cleaner and more tender than non-kosher chickens.

ORGANIC There are no federal standards yet. In California, a chicken can be called organic if it has only consumed seed grown in soil that has been free of chemical pesticides and fertilizers for at least three years. Contact your state commissioner or secretary of agriculture for information about your state.

POUSSINS Only four to six weeks old, these chickens weigh from three quarters to one and one quarter pounds. Very tender and juicy, they make great single servings.

ROASTERS Larger than fryers and usually three to five months old. Roasters are more flavorful and have the highest ratio of meat to bone.

SQUAB A very young chicken weighing about one pound.

STEWING CHICKENS Mature female chickens more than ten months old and weighing four to five pounds. They need to be simmered in a soup or braising liquid until tender.

YOUNG ROASTERS Large meaty birds, three to five months old, these weigh five to eight pounds, and are best roasted or braised since they are not as tender as younger birds.

CHICKEN GLOSSARY

WEIGHTS

Ounces and Pounds	Metric Equivalent
¼ ounce	7 grams
⅓ ounce	10 g
½ ounce	14 g
1 ounce	28 g
1½ ounces	42 g
1¾ ounces	50 g
2 ounces	57 g
3 ounces	85 g
3½ ounces	100 g
4 ounces (¼ pound)	114 g
6 ounces	170 g
8 ounces (½ pound)	227 g
9 ounces	250 g
16 ounces (1 pound)	464 g

TEMPERATURE

°F (*Fahrenheit*)	°C (*Centigrade or Celsius*)
32 (water freezes)	0
200	95
212 (water boils)	100
250	120
275	135
300 (slow oven)	150
325	160
350 (moderate oven)	175
375	190
400 (hot oven)	205
425	220
450 (very hot oven)	232
475	245
500 (extremely hot oven)	260

LIQUID MEASURES

tsp.: teaspoon / Tbs.: tablespoon

Spoons and Cups	Metric Equivalents
¼ tsp.	1.23 milliliters
½ tsp.	2.5 ml
¾ tsp.	3.7 ml
1 tsp.	5 ml
1 dessertspoon	10 ml
1 Tbs. (3 tsp.)	15 ml
2 Tbs. (1 ounce)	30 ml
¼ cup	60 ml
⅓ cup	80 ml
½ cup	120 ml
⅔ cup	160 ml
¾ cup	180 ml
1 cup (8 ounces)	240 ml
2 cups (1 pint)	480 ml
3 cups	720 ml
4 cups (1 quart)	1 liter
4 quarts (1 gallon)	3.75 liters

LENGTH

U.S. Measurements	Metric Equivalent
⅛ inch	3 mm
¼ inch	6 mm
⅜ inch	1 cm
½ inch	1.2 cm
¾ inch	2 cm
1 inch	2.5 cm
1¼ inches	3.1 cm
1½ inches	3.7 cm
2 inches	5 cm
3 inches	7.5 cm
4 inches	10 cm
5 inches	12.5 cm

APPROXIMATE EQUIVALENTS

1 kilo is slightly more than 2 pounds
1 liter is slightly more than 1 quart
1 meter is slightly over 3 feet
1 centimeter is approximately ⅜ inch

SUMMER CHICKEN

INDEX

SUMMER • WINTER

CHICKEN

LORI LONGBOTHAM

Photography by

MELANIE ACEVEDO

QUILL

WILLIAM MORROW AND COMPANY

NEW YORK

Library of Congress Cataloging-in-Publication Data
Longbotham, Lori.
Summer / winter chicken / Lori Longbotham.
p.   cm.
ISBN 0-688-15212-0
1. Cookery (Chicken)   I. Title.
TX750. C45L66   1997
641.6'65--dc21
97-6247
CIP

ISBN: 0-688-15212-0

Editor: DEBORAH MINTCHEFF
Designer: SUSI OBERHELMAN
Assistant Editor: SARAH STEWART
Assistant Designer: AYAKO HOSONO
Food Stylist: KEVIN CRAFTS
Prop Stylist: ROBYN GLASER

First Edition

1   2   3   4   5   6   7   8   9   10

PRODUCED BY SMALLWOOD & STEWART, INC., NEW YORK CITY

PRINTED IN SINGAPORE

WINTER CHICKEN
CONTENTS

CHICKEN

WINTER

INTRODUCTION

Like most people, my approach to cooking changes in the colder months. Where in summer I looked for lighter flavors, in winter I crave heartier dishes; in place of salads I long for warming soups and stews. And my philosophy alters as much as my palate: now I relish the warmth and comfort of the kitchen, richer ingredients, more complex dishes. The chicken recipes that follow meet all these requirements, using ingredients such as hearty red wine, dried mushrooms, and winter citrus fruit, combined with heady flavorings like ginger, cinnamon, honey, and hoisin sauce to create comforting winter dishes. From soups, gumbos, and pot pies that warm us to flavorful paellas, tagines, and stews that fill the house with delicious aromas, here are dozens of ways to create satisfying meals on even the coldest night.

CHANGING SEASONS: HOW TO USE THIS BOOK

When you feel like moving on to summer dishes, just flip the book over and you'll find a whole new set of recipes tailored to warm-weather dining. Each half is a mini book unto itself, complete with its own page numbers and index.

W I N T E R
CHICKEN

OLD-FASHIONED CHICKEN NOODLE SOUP

Serves 8

THIS WILL CURE WHAT AILS YOU. IT'S THE QUINTESSENTIAL CHICKEN SOUP. IF YOU'VE GOT A BIG ENOUGH POT, MAKE A DOUBLE BATCH JUST UP TO THE POINT OF ADDING THE NOODLES. STORE IT IN THE FREEZER IN PORTION-SIZED CONTAINERS—IT'S GREAT TO HAVE ON HAND.

1 (3½- to 4-pound) chicken, quartered

About 10 cups cold water

6 large carrots, thinly sliced

3 celery stalks, coarsely chopped

3 unpeeled parsnips, coarsely chopped

1 large onion, chopped

1 unpeeled medium-size turnip, chopped

2 garlic cloves

10 fresh parsley sprigs

4 fresh dill sprigs

Salt

Freshly ground pepper

8 ounces fine, medium, or wide egg noodles

1 tablespoon each chopped fresh parsley, dill & snipped chives, for garnish

Put the chicken into a large pot and add enough of the cold water to cover. Bring to a boil over high heat, skimming off any froth that rises to the surface. Set aside 2 cups of the carrots. Add the remaining carrots to the pot along with the celery, parsnips, onion, turnip, garlic, parsley, dill sprigs, and 1½ teaspoons salt. Simmer, partially covered, for about 1 hour, or until the chicken is cooked through.

Remove the chicken to a plate and when cool enough to handle, remove the skin and bones, reserving them, and cut or tear the meat into bite-size pieces. Cover and set aside. Add the chicken skin and bones to the broth and continue to cook, partially covered, for 20 minutes.

Pour the soup through a fine-mesh strainer set over a large saucepan, pressing on the solids with the back of a wooden spoon . Add the reserved carrots and season with salt and pepper. Bring to a simmer and cook, covered, for 10 minutes, or until the carrots are crisp-tender. Add the egg noodles and cook according to the package directions, until just tender. Add the chicken to the pan and heat through.

To serve, ladle the soup into bowls and garnish with the chopped parsley, dill, and chives.

CLASSIC
HOT-AND-SOUR SOUP

6 dried Chinese black mushrooms soaked in ⅔ cup boiling water for 20 minutes

2½ tablespoons cornstarch

2 boneless skinless chicken breast halves (about 10 ounces), cut into long thin strips

2 tablespoons soy sauce

1 tablespoon Shaoxing wine* or dry sherry

5 cups chicken broth

6 ounces firm tofu, cut into ½-x-1½-inch strips

Salt

3 tablespoons rice or cider vinegar, or more to taste

1½ tablespoons minced peeled fresh ginger, or more to taste

1½ teaspoons Asian sesame oil, or more to taste

Freshly ground pepper

2 large eggs, lightly beaten

2 tablespoons minced scallion (green part only), for garnish

Fresh cilantro leaves, for garnish

*Shaoxing wine is available in liquor stores and some Asian markets.

SOUP DOESN'T GET BETTER THAN THIS. CORNSTARCH LENDS A SILKY QUALITY TO THE STOCK AND THE INGREDIENTS CONTRIBUTE ALL THE RIGHT FLAVORS AND TEXTURES TO MAKE THIS SOUP TRULY SATISFYING.

Remove the mushrooms, reserving the liquid; rinse and dry. Remove the stems and cut the mushrooms into thin slices. Set aside. Pour the mushroom liquid through a paper towel–lined strainer set over a small bowl.

In a medium-size bowl, combine 2 tablespoons of the mushroom liquid and 1½ teaspoons of the cornstarch. Add the chicken, 1 tablespoon of the soy sauce, and the wine, tossing until well coated. Set aside.

In a small dish, stir together 3 tablespoons of the mushroom liquid and the remaining 2 tablespoons cornstarch until well blended. Set aside. Discard the remaining mushroom liquid or save for another use.

In a large heavy saucepan, bring the broth to a boil over medium-high heat. Add the chicken mixture and mushrooms and boil, stirring, for 1 minute. Add the tofu and the remaining 1 tablespoon soy sauce, and season with salt. Return to a boil, skimming off any froth that rises to the surface. Stir in the cornstarch mixture and cook, stirring constantly, for about 30 seconds, or until smooth and thickened. Stir in the vinegar, ginger, and sesame oil, and season with pepper. Remove the soup from the heat and add the eggs in a slow steady stream, stirring the soup once in a circular motion. Taste and add more vinegar, ginger, and/or sesame oil, if desired. Ladle the soup into bowls and garnish with the scallion and cilantro.

CHICKEN SOUP
WITH SWISS CHARD

Serves 6

INSPIRED BY A CLASSIC PORTUGUESE SOUP, THIS
HEARTY DISH WILL KEEP YOUR INSIDES WARM WHEN IT'S
TOO COLD OUTSIDE. IT'S ALSO LOADED WITH
BETA CAROTENE AND LOTS OF GOOD-FOR-YOU GREENS.

2 tablespoons fruity olive oil

¼ pound chorizo, thinly sliced

2 boneless skinless chicken
thighs (about ¾ pound),
cut into 1-inch-long strips

1 large red onion, chopped

2 garlic cloves, cut into quarters

2 large sweet potatoes, peeled
& thinly sliced

4 cups chicken broth

Salt

Crushed red pepper flakes

2 cups packed julienned
Swiss chard leaves

In a Dutch oven, heat the oil over medium-high heat. Cook the chorizo, stirring, for 2 minutes, or until browned. Remove to a medium-size bowl. Add the chicken to the pot and cook, stirring, for about 3 minutes, or until browned; remove to the bowl. Add the onion and garlic to the pot and cook, stirring occasionally, for 3 minutes, or until softened. Add the sweet potatoes and broth. Season with salt and red pepper flakes and bring to a boil. Reduce the heat and simmer, covered, for 20 minutes, or until the sweet potatoes are very soft.

In a blender, puree the sweet potato mixture in small batches. Wash out the Dutch oven and return the sweet potato puree to the pot. Add the chorizo and chicken and simmer for 5 minutes. Add the Swiss chard and simmer for 5 minutes longer, or until tender and bright green. Season with salt and red pepper flakes.

Ladle the soup into large deep bowls and serve.

CHICKEN & SAUSAGE GUMBO

2 large red onions, sliced

½ pound small okra, halved

1 large yellow bell pepper, halved, cored, seeded & chopped

1 cup chopped celery, including some leaves

¼ cup minced fresh parsley

2 bay leaves

4 garlic cloves, thinly sliced

2 teaspoons fresh thyme leaves

½ teaspoon ground allspice

2 teaspoons salt

1 teaspoon each ground red & freshly ground black pepper

¾ pound andouille sausage, sliced

8 chicken thighs (about 2 pounds)

Vegetable oil

⅔ cup all-purpose flour

1 (6-ounce) can tomato paste

2 quarts chicken broth or water

1 (16-ounce) can whole tomatoes, drained & chopped

½ cup minced scallions

1 tablespoon white vinegar

Hot cooked rice, for serving

THE NAME GUMBO COMES FROM AN AFRICAN WORD FOR OKRA, A KEY INGREDIENT IN THIS CREOLE STEW. THE ROUX, AN ESSENTIAL PART OF THE GUMBO, SHOULD BE COOKED FOR ABOUT THIRTY MINUTES, OR UNTIL IT IS A RICH HAZELNUT BROWN COLOR.

In a large bowl, combine the onion, okra, bell pepper, celery, and ¼ cup of the parsley. Add the bay leaves, garlic, thyme, allspice, salt, ground red and black pepper, tossing until well combined.

In a large Dutch oven, cook the sausage over medium heat, for about 6 minutes, or until beginning to brown. Remove to a large bowl. Cook the chicken in batches, beginning with the skin side down, for about 5 minutes on each side, or until browned. Remove to the bowl.

Pour all the fat from the Dutch oven into a glass measuring cup and add enough vegetable oil to equal ⅔ cup. Return the oil to the pot and cook over medium-low heat, scraping to loosen any browned bits in the bottom of the pot. Gradually stir in the flour and cook, stirring, for about 30 minutes, or until the roux is a very dark rich brown, but not burned. Immediately add the vegetable mixture and cook, stirring, for 2 minutes. Blend the tomato paste with 1 cup of the broth. Add to the pot along with the sausage, chicken, tomatoes, and the remaining 7 cups broth. Bring to a boil. Reduce the heat and simmer for 1 hour, or until the gumbo is thickened. Stir in the scallions and vinegar. Remove from the heat and let stand for 10 minutes. Ladle into large bowls along with the rice and serve.

CHICKEN WITH BACON & GOAT CHEESE

Serves 4

I LOVE THE COMBINATION OF FLAVORS IN THIS VERY SATISFYING AND COMFORTING DISH. GOAT CHEESE AND CREAM MAKE A SCRUMPTIOUS SAUCE FOR THE CHICKEN AND IT'S VERY INVITING SERVED WITH A SIDE DISH OF POTATOES COOKED ANY STYLE.

2 slices bacon, cut into ¼-inch-wide strips

¼ cup all-purpose flour

Salt & freshly ground pepper

4 boneless skinless chicken breast halves (about 5 ounces each)

2 tablespoons unsalted butter

½ cup heavy cream

1 shallot, minced

2 tablespoons mild goat cheese, such as Montrachet

1 tablespoon fresh lemon juice, or to taste

¼ cup minced watercress leaves

Cook the bacon in a large cast-iron or other heavy skillet just until crisp. Remove and drain on a paper towel-lined plate.

On a plate, combine the flour, ½ teaspoon salt, and ½ teaspoon pepper. Lightly coat the chicken breasts with the flour, shaking off the excess.

Wipe out the bacon pan. Melt the butter in the skillet over medium heat. Cook the chicken, turning once, for 10 to 12 minutes, or until browned and cooked through. Remove to a plate and cover to keep warm.

Pour the cream into the skillet and increase the heat to medium-high. Deglaze the skillet by bringing the cream to a boil and scraping to loosen any browned bits in bottom of the pan. Add the shallot and cook, stirring frequently, for about 4 minutes, or until the cream has thickened. Add the goat cheese, lemon juice, and half the watercress, stirring until thoroughly blended and heated through. Season with salt and pepper.

To serve, place the chicken breasts on serving plates, spoon the sauce over, and sprinkle with the remaining watercress and the bacon.

CHICKEN WITH
LEMON & HERBS

½ cup all-purpose flour

Salt & freshly ground pepper

4 boneless skinless chicken breast
    halves (about 5 ounces each)

2 tablespoons unsalted butter

½ cup heavy cream

½ cup chicken broth

2 shallots, minced

1 tablespoon grated lemon zest

2 teaspoons fresh thyme leaves

1 teaspoon minced fresh
    tarragon, plus whole sprigs,
    for garnish

2 tablespoons fresh lemon juice,
    or to taste

THIS JUST MIGHT BECOME A STANDARD AT YOUR
HOUSE THE WAY IT IS AT MINE. THE FLAVORS MAKE IT A
SATISFYING DISH AT ANY TIME OF THE YEAR.

On a plate, combine the flour, ½ teaspoon salt, and ½ teaspoon pepper. Lightly coat the chicken breasts with the flour, shaking off the excess.

In a large cast-iron or other heavy skillet, melt the butter over medium heat. Cook the chicken, turning once, for 8 to 10 minutes, or until cooked through. Remove to a plate and cover to keep warm.

Pour the cream and broth into the skillet and increase the heat to medium high. Deglaze the skillet by bringing the cream mixture to a boil and scraping to loosen any browned bits in the bottom of the skillet. Add the shallots, lemon zest, thyme, and tarragon. Cook, stirring frequently, for 3 minutes, or until the sauce has thickened. Stir in the lemon juice and season with salt and pepper.

Place the chicken breasts on serving plates, spoon the sauce over, and garnish with the tarragon sprigs

HOISIN CHICKEN WITH SCALLIONS

¼ cup all-purpose flour

Salt & freshly ground pepper

4 boneless skinless chicken
   breast halves (about
   5 ounces each)

2 tablespoons canola or
   other vegetable oil

½ cup chicken broth

¼ cup plus 1 tablespoon minced
   scallions

2 tablespoons hoisin sauce

2 tablespoons julienned peeled
   fresh ginger

2 garlic cloves, thinly sliced

2 teaspoons soy sauce

½ teaspoon Asian sesame oil

Crushed red pepper flakes

½ teaspoon sesame seeds, toasted

HOISIN SAUCE IS A GREAT "CONVENIENCE FOOD" FROM YOUR SUPERMARKET SHELF—JUST A BIT WILL ADD LOTS OF INTENSE AUTHENTIC ASIAN FLAVOR TO A DISH. TRY AN IMPORTED BRAND—THEY ARE NOT NECESSARILY MORE EXPENSIVE, BUT ARE USUALLY OF BETTER QUALITY.

On a plate, combine the flour, ½ teaspoon salt, and ½ teaspoon pepper. Lightly coat the chicken breasts with the flour, shaking off the excess.

In a large cast-iron or other heavy skillet, heat the oil over medium heat. Cook the chicken, turning once, for 10 to 12 minutes, or until browned and cooked through. Remove to a plate and cover to keep warm.

Pour the broth into the skillet and increase the heat to medium-high. Deglaze the skillet by bringing the broth to a boil and scraping to loosen any browned bits in the bottom of the pan. Add ¼ cup of the scallions, the hoisin sauce, ginger, garlic, soy sauce, sesame oil, and red pepper flakes to taste to the skillet. Cook, stirring frequently, for 3 minutes, or until the sauce has thickened. Season with salt, if desired.

To serve, place the chicken breasts on serving plates, spoon the sauce over, and sprinkle with the remaining 1 tablespoon scallions and the sesame seeds.

SAUTEED CHICKEN WITH PEARS

Serves 4

SMOOTH AND CREAMY, WITH LOTS OF
FRESH FRUIT FLAVOR, THIS MAKES A LOVELY SUPPER DISH.
IF YOU PREFER TO USE SOUR CREAM,
WHISK IT IN AT THE END—IT CAN'T TAKE BOILING.

¼ cup all-purpose flour

Salt & freshly ground pepper

4 boneless skinless chicken breast halves (about 5 ounces each)

2 tablespoons unsalted butter

¼ cup pear juice or nectar

¼ cup chicken broth

¼ cup minced shallots

¼ cup crème fraîche or sour cream

1 teaspoon fresh lemon juice, or to taste

1 teaspoon packed light brown sugar

1 firm but ripe pear, peeled, halved, cored & cut into ½-inch dice

2 teaspoons minced fresh flat-leaf parsley, for garnish

On a plate, combine the flour, ½ teaspoon salt, and ½ teaspoon pepper. Lightly coat the chicken breasts with the flour, shaking off the excess.

In a large cast-iron or other heavy skillet, melt the butter over medium heat. Cook the chicken, turning once, for 10 to 12 minutes, or until browned and cooked through. Remove to a plate and cover to keep warm.

Pour the pear juice and broth into the skillet and increase the heat to medium-high. Deglaze the skillet by bringing the broth mixture to a boil and scraping to loosen any browned bits in the bottom of the pan. Add the shallots, crème fraîche, lemon juice, and brown sugar, and season with salt and pepper. Cook, stirring frequently, for 3 minutes, or until the sauce is slightly thickened. Stir in the pear and cook, stirring gently, for 1 minute.

To serve, place the chicken breasts on serving plates, spoon the sauce over, and sprinkle with the parsley.

CHICKEN WITH SAGE & DRIED CHERRIES

Serves 4

THIS IS ONE OF MY FAVORITE COMBINATIONS—I LOVE THE
WAY THE AROMATIC SAGE PLAYS OFF THE CHERRIES, RESULTING
IN A VERY COMPLEX FLAVOR FOR SUCH A SIMPLE DISH.
I BUY A WONDERFUL CHERRY JUICE AT MY LOCAL HEALTH FOOD
STORE; MADE BY THE R. W. KNUDSEN FAMILY IN CHICO,
CALIFORNIA, IT'S 100 PERCENT PURE UNSWEETENED CHERRY
JUICE AND HAS A VERY INTENSE FLAVOR.

¼ cup all-purpose flour

Salt & freshly ground pepper

4 boneless skinless chicken breast
halves (about 5 ounces each)

2 tablespoons unsalted butter

½ cup cherry juice, chicken
broth, or a combination

⅓ cup dried sour cherries

2 shallots, minced

1 garlic clove, thinly sliced

1 teaspoon packed dark
brown sugar

½ teaspoon finely shredded fresh
sage, plus whole sprigs,
for garnish

⅛ teaspoon ground allspice

On a plate, combine the flour, ½ teaspoon salt, and ½ teaspoon pepper.
Lightly coat the chicken breasts with the flour, shaking off the excess.

In a large cast-iron or other heavy skillet, melt the butter over medium heat. Cook the chicken, turning once, for 10 to 12 minutes, or until
browned and cooked through. Remove to a plate and cover to keep warm.

Pour the cherry juice into the skillet and increase the heat to medium-high. Deglaze the skillet by bringing the cherry juice to a boil and
scraping to loosen any browned bits in the bottom of the pan. Add the
dried cherries, shallots, garlic, brown sugar, sage, and allspice and cook,
stirring frequently, for 3 minutes, or until the sauce is slightly thickened.
Season with salt and pepper.

To serve, place the chicken breasts on serving plates, spoon the sauce
over, and garnish with the sage sprigs.

CHICKEN WITH BACON & CABBAGE

4 slices bacon, cut into
 ¼-inch-wide strips

¼ cup all-purpose flour

Salt & freshly ground pepper

4 boneless skinless chicken breast
 halves (about 5 ounces each)

2 tablespoons unsalted butter

½ cup chicken broth

6 cups finely shredded Savoy
 cabbage

1 McIntosh apple, halved, cored
 & cut into thin wedges

1 tablespoon packed light
 brown sugar

1 teaspoon balsamic vinegar

1 bay leaf

1 teaspoon fresh thyme leaves

1 tablespoon snipped fresh
 chives, for garnish

THIS IS HEARTY WINTERTIME FARE WITH LONG-COOKED FLAVOR, BUT YOU WON'T BE SLAVING OVER THE STOVE FOR LONG—LESS THAN THE TIME IT WOULD TAKE TO MICROWAVE A FROZEN DINNER. THE BROWN SUGAR AND VINEGAR GIVE THE DISH A SATISFYING SWEET-AND-SOUR ELEMENT THAT BLENDS BEAUTIFULLY WITH THE CABBAGE, APPLE, AND FRESH HERBS.

Cook the bacon in a large cast-iron or other heavy skillet just until crisp. Remove the bacon to a paper towel–lined plate to drain, leaving the fat in the skillet. Set the pan aside.

On a plate, combine the flour, ½ teaspoon salt, and ½ teaspoon pepper. Lightly coat the chicken breasts with the flour, shaking off the excess.

In the same skillet, melt the butter over medium heat. Cook the chicken, turning once, for 10 to 12 minutes, or until browned and cooked through. Remove to a plate and cover to keep warm.

Pour the broth into the skillet and increase the heat to medium-high. Deglaze the skillet by bringing the broth to a boil and scraping to loosen any browned bits in the bottom of the pan. Add the cabbage, apple, brown sugar, vinegar, bay leaf, and thyme, and season with salt and pepper. Cook, stirring frequently, for about 10 minutes, or until the cabbage is very soft. Discard the bay leaf.

To serve, place the cabbage on serving plates, top with the chicken, and sprinkle with the bacon and chives.

CHICKEN WITH LEEKS & ORANGE

Serves 4

THE REFRESHING CITRUS TASTE OF ORANGE AND
THE SUBTLE PINE-LIKE QUALITY OF FRESH ROSEMARY MAKES
THIS A WINNING COMBINATION WITH CHICKEN.

On a plate, combine the flour, ½ teaspoon salt, and ½ teaspoon pepper. Lightly coat the chicken breasts with the flour, shaking off the excess.

In a large cast-iron or other heavy skillet, melt the butter over medium heat. Cook the chicken, turning once, for 10 to 12 minutes, or until browned and cooked through. Remove to a plate and cover to keep warm.

Pour the orange juice and broth into the skillet and increase the heat to medium-high. Deglaze the skillet by bringing the broth mixture to a boil and scraping to loosen any browned bits in the bottom of the pan. Add the leek, orange zest, and rosemary, and season with salt and pepper. Cook, stirring frequently, for 4 to 5 minutes, or until the sauce has thickened slightly. Discard the orange zest and rosemary sprig.

To serve, place the chicken breasts on serving plates, spoon the sauce over, and sprinkle with the parsley.

¼ cup all-purpose flour

Salt & freshly ground pepper

4 boneless skinless chicken breast halves (about 5 ounces each)

2 tablespoons unsalted butter

⅓ cup fresh orange juice

⅓ cup chicken broth

1 small leek (white part only), halved lengthwise, thinly sliced, washed thoroughly & dried

2 strips orange zest (removed with a vegetable peeler)

1 small fresh rosemary sprig

2 teaspoons minced fresh flat-leaf parsley, for garnish

BALSAMIC CHICKEN WITH THYME

¼ cup all-purpose flour

Salt & freshly ground pepper

4 boneless skinless chicken
   breast halves (about 5
   ounces each)

2 tablespoons olive oil

1 large red onion, thinly sliced

¾ cup chicken broth

2 tablespoons balsamic vinegar

1 teaspoon fresh thyme leaves,
   plus whole sprigs,
   for garnish

1 teaspoon minced fresh
   flat-leaf parsley

THIS RECIPE COULDN'T BE SIMPLER AND IS VERY FLAVORFUL. IT MAKES GREAT USE OF BALSAMIC VINEGAR, EFFECTIVELY TURNING IT INTO A SAUCE.

On a plate, combine the flour, ½ teaspoon salt, and ½ teaspoon pepper. Lightly coat the chicken breasts with the flour, shaking off the excess.

In a large cast-iron or other heavy skillet, heat the oil over medium heat. Cook the chicken, turning once, for 10 to 12 minutes, or until browned and cooked through. Remove to a plate and cover to keep warm.

Add the onion to the skillet and cook, stirring, for 1 minute, or until lightly browned. Add the broth, vinegar, and thyme, and season with salt and pepper. Bring to a boil and cook, stirring frequently, for 7 minutes, or until the onions are softened and the sauce is syrupy.

To serve, place the chicken breasts on serving plates, spoon the sauce over, and sprinkle with the parsley. Garnish with the thyme sprigs.

TEXAS CHICKEN
& DUMPLINGS

2 pounds boneless skinless
    chicken thighs

¼ cup all-purpose flour

Salt & freshly ground pepper

3 tablespoons vegetable oil

1 leek (white part only), thinly
    sliced, washed & dried

2 shallots, minced

1½ cups chicken broth

2 slender carrots, cut into
    ¼-inch-wide diagonal slices

2 celery stalks, cut into ¼-inch dice

½ cup apple cider or juice

1 bay leaf

1 teaspoon chopped fresh thyme

½ teaspoon minced fresh sage

PARSLEY DUMPLINGS

1⅓ cups all-purpose flour

2 teaspoons baking powder

¼ teaspoon salt

2 tablespoons minced fresh
    flat-leaf parsley

¾ cup plus 1 tablespoon milk

½ cup frozen tiny peas, thawed

THIS RECIPE IS AN ADAPTATION OF MY TEXAS GRANDMOTHER'S RECIPE AND, LIKE ALL HER FOOD, IS SOOTHING AND COMFORTING. IT'S ALSO A COMPLETE MEAL IN ONE, SO YOU WON'T NEED ANY SIDE DISHES.

Cut each chicken thigh lengthwise into 4 pieces. On a plate, combine the flour, ½ teaspoon salt, and ½ teaspoon pepper. Coat the chicken with the flour, shaking off the excess.

In a large heavy skillet, heat the oil over medium-high heat. Cook the chicken, in batches if necessary, for about 2 minutes on each side, or until lightly browned. Remove the chicken to a plate.

Add the leek and shallots to the skillet. Cook over medium heat for 2 minutes, or until softened. Add the chicken, broth, carrots, celery, cider, bay leaf, thyme, sage, ¼ teaspoon salt, and ¼ teaspoon pepper. Reduce the heat to medium-low and cook, partially covered, stirring occasionally, for 15 minutes, or until the carrots and celery are softened.

Meanwhile, prepare the parsley dumplings: Into a medium-size bowl, sift the flour, baking powder, and salt together 3 times. Stir in the parsley. Pour in the milk and stir with a wooden spoon just until blended.

Drop the dumplings by large spoonfuls into the simmering broth, making 12 dumplings. Cover and cook for 3 to 5 minutes, or until a toothpick inserted into the center of a dumpling comes out clean. Stir in the peas and discard the bay leaf.

Ladle the chicken and dumplings into large deep bowls and serve.

NORMANDY CHICKEN WITH APPLES

¼ cup (½ stick) unsalted butter

1 small red onion, cut into
    thin slices

1 Granny Smith apple, peeled,
    halved, cored & cut into
    thin wedges

¾ cup apple cider or juice

1 tablespoon Calvados,
    applejack, or brandy

4 boneless skinless chicken breast
    halves (about 5 ounces each)

Salt & freshly ground pepper

¼ cup half-and-half

½ teaspoon minced fresh
    tarragon, plus whole sprigs,
    for garnish

INSPIRED BY THE NORMANDY REGION OF FRANCE,
WHERE THEY HAVE SUPERB APPLES, CREAM, AND BUTTER, THIS
DISH WILL BE A HIT WITH FRIENDS AND FAMILY.
IT'S QUICK AND EASY ENOUGH FOR WEEKDAY DINNERS AND
SPECIAL ENOUGH FOR DINNER PARTIES.

In a large cast-iron or other heavy skillet, melt 3 tablespoons of the butter over medium-low heat. Add the onion and cook, stirring, for 5 minutes, or until softened. Stir in the apple, cider, and Calvados. Cook, stirring, over medium-high heat for about 12 minutes, or until the apple has softened. Using a slotted spoon, remove the apple and onion to a small bowl.

Increase the heat to high and cook for about 3 minutes, or until the pan liquid is very thick and brown. Add the pan liquid to the apples.

Season the chicken with salt and pepper. In the same skillet, melt the remaining 1 tablespoon butter over medium heat. Cook the chicken for 5 to 7 minutes on each side, or until dark golden brown and just cooked through. Remove the chicken to a platter and cover to keep warm.

Return the apple mixture to the skillet and add the half-and-half and tarragon. Season with salt and pepper and cook over medium-high heat, stirring, occasionally, for about 4 minutes, or until the juices have thickened.

To serve, spoon the apple mixture over the chicken, and garnish with the tarragon sprigs.

COQ AU VIN ROUGE

TO PEEL PEARL ONIONS FOR THIS DISH,
JUST DROP THEM INTO A SMALL SAUCEPAN OF BOILING
WATER FOR ONE MINUTE, DRAIN
IN A COLANDER, AND RINSE WITH COLD WATER.
THE SKINS WILL SLIP RIGHT OFF.

Cook the bacon in a Dutch oven until crisp. Remove the bacon to a a paper towel–lined plate, leaving the fat in the pot. Set the pot aside.

On a plate, combine ½ cup of the flour, 1 teaspoon salt, and ½ teaspoon pepper. Lightly coat the chicken with the seasoned flour, shaking off the excess.

In the Dutch oven, melt 3 tablespoons of the butter over medium-high heat. Cook the chicken, in batches, turning once, for about 5 minutes on each side, or until golden brown. Remove the chicken to a large bowl. Add the pearl onions, shallots, carrots, and garlic to the pot and cook, covered, stirring occasionally, for about 10 to 15 minutes, or until the onions are golden brown. Add the wine and broth and deglaze the pan by bringing the liquid to a boil and scraping up any browned bits in the bottom of the Dutch oven.

Preheat the oven to 200°F.

Return the chicken to the pot and add the bouquet garni. Cover, reduce the heat, and cook at a bare simmer for about 15 minutes, or until the breasts are just cooked through. Remove the breasts and wings to a large deep ovenproof serving platter, cover loosely, and keep warm in the

---

4 slices bacon, cut into ¼-inch-wide strips

½ cup plus 2 tablespoons all-purpose flour

Salt & freshly ground pepper

1 (3- to 3½-pound) chicken, cut into 8 pieces

6 tablespoons (¾ stick) unsalted butter

24 small pearl onions, peeled

8 shallots, thinly sliced

1 cup baby carrots

2 garlic cloves, coarsely chopped

2 cups dry red wine, preferably a Burgundy

1 cup chicken broth

Bouquet garni (5 sprigs each fresh thyme & parsley & 1 bay leaf, tied together with kitchen string)

16 small button mushrooms, stems removed, briefly rinsed & quartered

2 tablespoons Cognac or brandy

½ teaspoon fresh lemon juice, or to taste

1 tablespoon minced fresh flat-leaf parsley, for garnish

oven. Continue cooking the dark meat for about 10 minutes longer, or until the juices from the thigh run clear when pierced with a paring knife. Remove the chicken and carrots to the platter; return to the oven. Increase the heat to high and let the sauce boil for 10 minutes.

With a fork, mix 2 tablespoons of the butter with the remaining 2 tablespoons flour in a small bowl until blended. Reduce the heat to a simmer and add the butter-flour mixture, 1 tablespoon at a time, whisking, until the sauce is the consistency of light cream. (You may not need to use all of the butter-flour mixture.)

In a small skillet, melt the remaining 1 tablespoon butter over medium heat. Add the mushrooms and cook, stirring, for about 5 minutes, or until they have absorbed their liquid and are lightly browned. Add the Cognac and, standing back, ignite with a long match, shaking the skillet until the flames subside. Season with salt and pepper and the lemon juice.

Discard the bouquet garni. To serve, spoon the mushrooms around the chicken, pour the sauce over, and sprinkle with the bacon and parsley.

CHICKEN WITH GINGER & LENTILS

½ cup all-purpose flour

8 chicken thighs (about 2 pounds), skin removed

2 tablespoons canola or other vegetable oil

1 cup French green or brown lentils

6 large scallions, chopped

¼ cup plus 2 tablespoons minced fresh cilantro

2 tablespoons minced fresh flat-leaf parsley

6 dried peaches, quartered

⅓ cup each dried sour cherries & golden raisins

½ teaspoon minced peeled fresh ginger

½ teaspoon ground cinnamon

¼ teaspoon each ground allspice & red pepper

½ teaspoon salt

2 cups chicken broth

PERFECT FOR A COZY SUNDAY SUPPER, THIS DISH HAS GREAT FLAVOR AND INCLUDES MANY HEALTHFUL INGREDIENTS. FIBER AND NUTRIENTS ARE PROVIDED BY THE LENTILS, DRIED PEACHES, CHERRIES, AND RAISINS.

Preheat the oven to 350° F.

Spread the flour on a plate and lightly coat the chicken with the flour, shaking off the excess.

In a large Dutch oven, heat the oil over medium heat. Cook the chicken, in batches, for about 5 minutes on each side, or until browned; remove to a large plate. Add the lentils, scallions, ¼ cup of the cilantro, the parsley, peaches, cherries, raisins, ginger, cinnamon, allspice, ground red pepper, and salt to the pot. Cook, stirring frequently, for 2 minutes. Place the chicken on top of the lentil mixture, pour the broth over, and bring to a boil over high heat.

Cover and bake for 30 minutes. Uncover and bake for 20 minutes longer, or until the chicken is cooked through and the lentils are tender. Sprinkle with the remaining 2 tablespoons cilantro and serve.

CHICKEN WITH FORTY GARLIC CLOVES

Serves 4

THE GARLIC IN THIS CLASSIC DISH FROM PROVENCE
GETS SO SWEET, SO SOFT, AND SO LUSCIOUS YOU MAY FIND
THAT FORTY CLOVES AREN'T ENOUGH. THE WARM
CROUTES ARE THE PERFECT ACCOMPANIMENT BECAUSE YOU
CAN SQUEEZE THE MELTED GARLIC FROM ITS PEEL,
SPREAD IT ON THE TOAST, AND EAT IT IN BLISS. USE THE
FRESHEST GARLIC YOU CAN FIND.

1 celery stalk with leaves,
   halved crosswise

6 fresh flat-leaf parsley sprigs

6 fresh thyme sprigs

3 fresh sage sprigs

3 fresh rosemary sprigs

1 bay leaf

1 (3- to 3½-pound) chicken

¼ cup fruity olive oil

Salt & freshly ground pepper

40 garlic cloves, unpeeled

Eight ½-inch-thick slices French
   bread, toasted & buttered,
   for serving

Preheat the oven to 375°F.

Place the celery, 3 sprigs each of the parsley and thyme, the sage, rosemary, and bay leaf in the chicken cavity. Put the chicken into a Dutch oven just large enough to hold it. Drizzle the oil over the chicken, turning to coat with the oil, and season with salt and pepper. Scatter the garlic cloves, the remaining 3 parsley sprigs, and the remaining 3 thyme sprigs around the chicken.

Roast the chicken, tightly covered, for 1½ hours, or until the juices from the thigh run clear when pierced with a paring knife.

To serve, bring the pot to the table so that the perfume of garlic and herbs is released when you remove the lid. Cut the chicken into serving pieces, arrange on a platter with the garlic, and serve the toasts on the side.

CHICKEN WITH SAFFRON & CORIANDER

¼ cup (½ stick) unsalted butter

6 small red onions, thinly sliced

2 garlic cloves

Salt & freshly ground pepper

1 bay leaf

1 teaspoon ground ginger

¼ teaspoon saffron threads, crumbled

¼ teaspoon each ground coriander & cumin

Pinch of ground cinnamon

8 chicken thighs (about 2 pounds), skin removed

1 cup chicken broth

1 cup cooked chickpeas, drained & rinsed if canned

1 tablespoon each minced fresh flat-leaf parsley & cilantro

Hot cooked rice, for serving

YOU CAN TOSS THIS DISH TOGETHER AND HAVE IT ON THE TABLE MUCH MORE QUICKLY THAN ITS LONG-SIMMERED TASTE INDICATES. THE MIX OF SPICES IS TYPICAL OF MOROCCO, WHERE THE FOOD OFTEN HAS A DEEP, COMPLEX FLAVOR BUT ISN'T COMPLICATED TO PREPARE.

In a large skillet, melt the butter over medium heat. Add the onions and garlic, and season with salt and pepper. Cook, stirring occasionally, for 5 minutes, or until the onions are softened. Add the bay leaf, ginger, saffron, coriander, cumin, and cinnamon and cook, stirring, for 3 minutes. Remove the onions to a plate. Add the chicken to the skillet and cook, turning once, for 10 minutes, or until it begins to brown.

Add the broth, increase the heat to high, and deglaze the pan by bringing the broth to a boil and scraping to loosen any browned bits in the bottom of the pan. Return the onions to the pan, and return to a boil. Reduce the heat, cover, and simmer the chicken, turning once, for about 20 minutes, or until it is just cooked through. Remove the chicken to a serving plate and cover to keep warm.

Increase the heat to high and stir in the chickpeas, parsley, and cilantro. Boil, uncovered, for 5 minutes, or until the sauce is slightly thickened. Season with salt and pepper and discard the bay leaf.

To serve, spoon the sauce over the chicken and serve with the rice.

CHICKEN IN DARK BEER WITH THYME

Serves 4

THIS DISH HAS HUGE, HEARTY FLAVORS
AND MAKES A SATISFYING COLD-WEATHER SUPPER. THE
CHICKEN, DARK BEER, DARK BROWN
SUGAR, AND THYME CREATE AN UNUSUAL ENTREE THAT WILL
APPEAL TO JUST ABOUT ANYONE.

¼ cup (½ stick) unsalted butter

4 whole chicken legs with thighs
(about 2 pounds) or 1
(3- to 3½-pound) chicken,
cut into 8 pieces

3 small leeks (white part only),
thinly sliced, washed
thoroughly & dried

4 shallots, finely chopped

½ teaspoon caraway seeds,
lightly crushed

1 (12-ounce) bottle dark beer

3 tablespoons packed dark
brown sugar

1 teaspoon fresh thyme leaves

Salt & freshly ground pepper

Hot cooked egg noodles,
for serving

1 tablespoon snipped
fresh chives

In a large skillet, melt the butter over medium heat. Add the chicken and cook, in batches if necessary, turning once, for about 10 minutes, or until golden brown. Remove the chicken to a plate and set aside.

Add the leeks, shallots, and caraway seeds to the pan and cook, scraping to loosen any browned bits in the bottom of the pan, for 10 minutes, or until the leeks are softened and just beginning to brown.

Return the chicken to the pan, add the beer, brown sugar, and thyme, and season with salt and pepper. Simmer, covered, for about 20 minutes, or until the chicken is just cooked through. Transfer the chicken to a large plate and cover to keep warm.

Increase the heat to high and boil the pan liquid for about 8 minutes, or until slightly thickened.

To serve, place the egg noodles on a platter, top with the chicken, pour the pan sauce over, and sprinkle with the chives.

CHICKEN TAGINE WITH PRUNES & ALMONDS

2 garlic cloves, mashed to a paste with ¾ teaspoon salt

2 teaspoons ground cumin

1 teaspoon coriander

1 teaspoon ground ginger

½ teaspoon ground red pepper

¼ teaspoon saffron threads, crumbled

8 chicken thighs (about 2 pounds), skin removed

3 tablespoons fruity olive oil

2 large red onions, thinly sliced

1-inch piece cinnamon stick

1½ cups chicken broth

1 tablespoon honey, preferably dark

¾ teaspoon Asian sesame oil

18 large pitted prunes

Hot cooked couscous, for serving

¼ cup chopped natural almonds, toasted, for garnish

Fresh cilantro leaves, for garnish

MOROCCO BOASTS SOME OF THE BEST FOOD IN THE WORLD AND DISPLAYS A GENIUS FOR EXOTIC FLAVOR COMBINATIONS SUCH AS PRUNES, ALMONDS, HONEY, AND SPICES. IN MOROCCO, TAGINES ARE PUT ON TO COOK IN A POT OF THE SAME NAME OVER CHARCOAL BRAZIERS EARLY IN THE MORNING. THEY ARE READY TO EAT WHEN LUNCHTIME COMES AND HUNGRY CUSTOMERS, FRIENDS, OR FAMILY ARRIVE.

In a small bowl, combine the garlic paste, cumin, coriander, ginger, ground red pepper, and saffron, mixing well. Place the chicken thighs on a baking sheet and rub with the spice mixture. Cover and refrigerate for 1 hour.

In a large Dutch oven, heat the oil over medium heat. Cook the chicken, in batches, for about 5 minutes on each side, or until browned. Remove to a large bowl.

Add the onions and cinnamon stick to the pot and cook, stirring occasionally, for 5 minutes, or until the onions are softened. Add the broth, honey, and sesame oil and cook for 2 minutes, scraping to loosen any browned bits in the bottom of the pot. Return the chicken to the pot and simmer, covered, for 30 minutes, until cooked through, adding the prunes for the last 3 minutes. Discard the cinnamon stick.

To serve, place the couscous on a large platter. Top with the chicken, pour the sauce over, and garnish with the almonds and cilantro.

CHICKEN & SHRIMP JAMBALAYA

Serves 6

THE WORD *JAMBALAYA* IS DERIVED FROM *JAMBON*, THE FRENCH WORD FOR HAM, AND *YA*, WHICH MEANS RICE IN AN AFRICAN DIALECT. THIS PARTICULAR JAMBALAYA IS A WONDERFUL CONGLOMERATION OF CHICKEN, SAUSAGES, AND SEAFOOD COOKED WITH RICE.

- 3 tablespoons canola or other vegetable oil
- ½ pound andouille or other garlic sausage, cut into ¼-inch-thick slices
- 4 boneless skinless chicken thighs (about 1¼ pounds), cut into thin strips
- 2 large onions, chopped
- 1 yellow bell pepper, halved, cored, seeded & chopped
- 8 scallions, chopped
- ¼ cup minced fresh flat-leaf parsley
- 4 garlic cloves, minced
- 2 bay leaves
- 1 (16-ounce) can whole tomatoes, undrained
- ¼ teaspoon dried thyme
- ¼ teaspoon each ground cumin, allspice & red pepper
- Pinch of ground cloves
- Salt & freshly ground pepper
- 1 cup long-grain white rice
- 2 cups chicken broth or water
- 1 pound small or medium-size shrimp, peeled & deveined

In a Dutch oven, heat the oil over medium heat until hot but not smoking. Add the sausage and cook, stirring, for 5 minutes, or until browned on the edges. Remove to a large bowl. Cook the chicken in batches, stirring, for about 10 minutes, or until golden brown. Add the chicken to the sausage.

Add the onions, bell pepper, three quarters of the scallions, 3 tablespoons of the parsley, the garlic, and bay leaves to the Dutch oven. Cook, stirring, for 5 minutes, scraping to loosen any browned bits in the bottom of the pot. Add the tomatoes and their juice, the thyme, cumin, allspice, ground red pepper, cloves, 1 teaspoon salt and ¼ teaspoon pepper. Cook, stirring, for 3 minutes, breaking up the tomatoes with a wooden spoon. Return the sausage and chicken to the Dutch oven, stir in the rice and broth, and bring to a boil over medium-high heat.

Reduce the heat to low and simmer, covered, without stirring, for 30 minutes, or until the rice is tender. The rice should be moist, not soupy.

Remove from the heat, stir in the shrimp, season with salt and pepper, and let stand, covered, for 10 minutes. Discard the bay leaves.

To serve, ladle the jambalaya into deep bowls and sprinkle with the remaining scallions and 1 tablespoon parsley.

CHICKEN WITH LEMON, CUMIN & MINT

Serves 4

Zest of 1 lemon, removed in
thin strips (with a vegetable
peeler)

½ cup fresh lemon juice

⅓ cup olive oil

2 tablespoons shredded fresh
mint, plus small sprigs,
for garnish

2 garlic cloves, minced

½ teaspoon hot paprika

½ teaspoon ground cumin

¼ teaspoon salt

¼ teaspoon freshly ground
pepper

4 boneless skinless chicken
thighs (about 1¼ pounds),
cut in half lengthwise

4 chicken wings, wing tips
cut off & discarded

Lemon wedges, for garnish

WITH GREAT AROMA AND FLAVOR, THIS IS A
GOOD EXAMPLE OF WHAT YOU MIGHT BE SERVED IN THE
MIDDLE EAST. IT'S SIMPLE TO PUT
TOGETHER AND MAKES A SATISFYING QUICK DINNER.

In a large bowl, combine the lemon zest, lemon juice, oil, 1 tablespoon of the mint, half the garlic, the paprika, cumin, salt, and pepper. Add the chicken, turning to coat. Cover and refrigerate for 40 minutes, turning the chicken occasionally.

Preheat the broiler.

Broil the chicken, 5 to 6 inches from the heat, for 5 minutes on each side, or until well browned and cooked through.

Transfer the chicken to a platter and sprinkle with the remaining 1 tablespoon mint and the garlic. Garnish with the mint sprigs and lemon wedges and serve.

DRUMSTICKS WITH GARLIC & HERBS

3 strips each lemon & orange
   zest (removed with a
   vegetable peeler)

¾ cup fresh orange juice

2 tablespoons fruity olive oil

½ teaspoon ground coriander

Salt & freshly ground pepper

8 chicken drumsticks (about
   2 pounds)

1 tablespoon chopped fresh
   flat-leaf parsley

2 teaspoons grated lemon zest

¼ teaspoon grated orange zest

1 small garlic clove, minced

3 small fresh basil leaves

THE GARLIC-AND-HERB MIXTURE IN THIS
DISH IS REALLY A GUSSIED-UP GREMOLATA. GREMOLATA IS
USUALLY PREPARED WITH MINCED LEMON ZEST,
PARSLEY, AND GARLIC. I'VE ADDED FINELY JULIENNED BASIL
AND ORANGE—IT'S A TASTY COMBINATION.

In a large bowl, whisk together the strips of lemon and orange zest, orange juice, oil, coriander, and salt and pepper. Add the drumsticks and turn to coat. Cover and marinate in the refrigerate for 1 hour, turning the chicken occasionally.

Preheat the broiler.

Transfer the drumsticks to a plate. Pour the marinade through a strainer into a small saucepan and bring to a boil over high heat. Remove from the heat.

Broil the chicken, 5 to 6 inches from the heat, for 10 minutes. Turn the chicken over, baste with the reserved marinade, and broil for 8 to 10 minutes longer, or until the juices run clear when the chicken is pierced with a paring knife; watching to make sure the chicken doesn't burn.

Meanwhile, chop together the parsley, grated lemon and orange zest, and the garlic, and transfer to a small bowl. Use a large knife to finely shred the basil leaves.

To serve, arrange the drumsticks on a platter, sprinkle with the parsley mixture, and top with the basil.

CHICKEN BREASTS WITH CHUTNEY BUTTER

Serves 4

JUST A BIT OF A FLAVORED BUTTER CAN
REALLY MAKE A DIFFERENCE. ONLY ONE AND A HALF
TABLESPOONS OF THIS CHUTNEY BUTTER
MAKES PLAIN GRILLED CHICKEN BREAST EXTRAORDINARY.

2 tablespoons chopped store-bought mango chutney

2 tablespoons unsalted butter, at room temperature

2 teaspoons minced fresh cilantro, plus whole sprigs, for garnish

¼ teaspoon ground red pepper

4 boneless skinless chicken breast halves (about 5 ounces each)

2 tablespoons canola or other vegetable oil

Salt & freshly ground pepper

Place a stovetop grill pan over medium heat or preheat a grill to hot and brush with oil.

In a small bowl, stir together the chutney, butter, 1 teaspoon of the cilantro, and the ground red pepper until smooth. Cover and refrigerate until ready to serve.

Put the chicken on a plate and drizzle with the oil, turning to coat evenly. Sprinkle with the remaining 1 teaspoon cilantro and season with salt and pepper.

Grill the chicken, turning once, for 5 to 7 minutes on each side, or until cooked through.

To serve, place the chicken on serving plates, top each with some chutney butter, and garnish with cilantro sprigs.

TUSCAN GRILLED CHICKEN

Serves 4

THIS CHICKEN TASTES AS IF IT WERE GRILLED OUTSIDE, AND THAT'S A GREAT THING IN THE MIDDLE OF WINTER. THERE'S NOTHING DIFFICULT ABOUT THE TECHNIQUE, YOU JUST HAVE TO BE CAREFUL NOT TO TEAR THE SKIN OF THE CHICKEN (BUT EVEN IF YOU DO, THE CHICKEN WILL STILL BE QUITE DELICIOUS—SO DON'T WORRY).

3 garlic cloves

Salt

1½ tablespoons minced fresh flat-leaf parsley

1½ tablespoons fresh thyme leaves

1 tablespoon extra-virgin olive oil

1 (3- to 3½-pound) chicken, patted dry

½ cup olive oil

½ teaspoon freshly ground pepper

½ teaspoon grated lemon zest

Lemon wedges, for garnish

Using a large knife, mince 2 of the garlic cloves. Sprinkle with ⅛ teaspoon salt and mash with the flat side of the knife until a paste forms. In a small bowl, combine the garlic mixture, 1 tablespoon of the parsley, 1 tablespoon of the thyme, and the extra-virgin olive oil. Set aside.

With kitchen scissors, cut off and discard the wing tips from the chicken. Split the chicken lengthwise, cutting through the breastbone. Lay the chicken out flat, skin side up. With the heel of your hand, press down firmly on the backbone, thighs, and leg joints to flatten the chicken. Beginning at the neck end, very gently slide your fingers under the skin to separate the skin from the meat. Spread the garlic-herb mixture evenly over the meat. Place the chicken on a platter, cover, and refrigerate for at least 1 hour or overnight.

In an 11-inch cast-iron or other heavy skillet, heat the olive oil over medium heat. Season the chicken with ½ teaspoon salt and the pepper. Place the chicken skin side down in the skillet. Place another heavy skillet (one that fits snugly inside the first skillet) on top of the chicken. Weight the skillet by placing several cans (the total weight should be about 7

pounds) inside the skillet. Cook the chicken for 20 minutes, turning the skillet several times to make sure the chicken doesn't stick to the bottom of the skillet.

Meanwhile, chop together the remaining 1½ teaspoons parsley and 1½ teaspoons thyme, the lemon zest, and the remaining garlic clove. Transfer to a small dish and set aside.

Remove the skillet from the top of the chicken. With a metal spatula, carefully loosen the chicken at one side and lift up. If the skin is not yet a deep rich brown color, cook for 5 minutes or so longer. With the spatula, lift the chicken (try not to tear the skin) and carefully turn it over. Cook for 8 to 10 minutes longer, or until the juices run clear when the thigh is pierced with a paring knife. Transfer the chicken to a cutting board; sprinkle with the herb mixture. Let stand, loosely covered, for 5 minutes.

Using poultry shears or a large knife, cut down along either side of the backbone and discard it. Cut the chicken into quarters and serve garnished with the lemon wedges.

ROSEMARY GRILLED CHICKEN

Serves 4

IN THE SUMMERTIME, TRY COOKING
THIS OUTDOORS ON THE GRILL—IT'S EQUALLY DELICIOUS. IN
FACT, THIS COULD BECOME ONE
OF YOUR FAVORITE WEEKLY MEALS ALL YEAR ROUND.

¼ cup fruity olive oil

Zest of 1 lemon (removed with a vegetable peeler)

1 tablespoon fresh lemon juice

1½ teaspoons minced fresh rosemary

1 teaspoon shredded fresh sage

2 garlic cloves, thinly sliced

½ teaspoon salt

¼ teaspoon freshly ground pepper

1 (3- to 3½-pound) chicken, cut into 8 pieces

Lemon wedges, for garnish

In a large bowl, combine the oil, lemon zest, lemon juice, rosemary, sage, and garlic, and season with salt and pepper. Add the chicken and turn to coat. Cover and marinate in the refrigerator for 1 hour, turning the chicken occasionally.

Preheat the broiler.

Broil the chicken, 5 to 6 inches from the heat, for 10 minutes. Turn the chicken over and broil for 8 to 10 minutes longer, or until the skin is browned and the juices from the thigh run clear when the chicken is pierced with a paring knife; watch the chicken carefully so that it does not burn.

Transfer the chicken to a platter. Serve hot, warm, or at room temperature, garnished with the lemon wedges.

FIVE-SPICE GRILLED CHICKEN

¼ cup hoisin sauce

1 tablespoon rice vinegar

1 tablespoon minced peeled
fresh ginger

1 teaspoon Asian sesame oil

½ teaspoon Chinese five-spice
powder

2 whole chicken breasts
(about 2¼ pounds), split

2 small scallions, minced

CHINESE FIVE-SPICE POWDER MAY INCLUDE CINNAMON, CLOVES, STAR ANISE, SZECHWAN PEPPERCORNS, NUTMEG, AND/OR FENNEL SEEDS, DEPENDING ON THE PARTICULAR BLEND. HIGH-QUALITY VERSIONS ARE AVAILABLE IN ASIAN MARKETS AND IN SUPERMARKETS.

In a large bowl, combine the hoisin sauce, vinegar, ginger, sesame oil, and five-spice powder. Add the chicken breasts and turn to coat. Cover and marinate in the refrigerator for 30 minutes, turning occasionally.

Preheat the broiler.

Broil the chicken, 5 to 6 inches from the heat, for 10 minutes. Turn the chicken over and broil for 8 to 10 minutes longer, or until the skin is browned and the juices run clear when pierced with a paring knife; watch the chicken carefully so that it does not burn.

To serve, transfer the chicken to a platter and sprinkle with the scallions.

QUICK CHICKEN PAELLA

Serves 4

HERE YOU HAVE ALL OF THE FLAVORS
OF A CLASSIC AND LONG-COOKING PAELLA IN A VERSION
THAT REQUIRES LESS THAN FIFTEEN
MINUTES ON THE STOVE. START COOKING THE RICE BEFORE
YOU BEGIN MAKING THE PAELLA.

Combine the saffron and chicken broth in a small bowl and set aside to steep.

In a large heavy skillet, heat the oil over medium-high heat. Add the shallots and cook, stirring, for 4 minutes, or until softened. Stir in the garlic and thyme and cook, stirring, for 1 minute. Stir in the bell peppers and tomatoes and cook, stirring, for 3 minutes. Add the chicken and the saffron mixture and cook, stirring, for 2 to 3 minutes, or until the chicken is just cooked through.

Remove the skillet from the heat and stir in the peas, ham, and lemon juice. Season with salt and pepper.

To serve, spoon the rice onto a serving platter, top with the paella, and sprinkle with the parsley.

Pinch of saffron threads, crumbled

¼ cup chicken broth, heated

2 tablespoons olive oil, preferably extra-virgin

½ cup sliced shallots

3 garlic cloves, minced

½ teaspoon fresh thyme leaves

1 each red & yellow bell pepper, halved, cored, seeded & cut into ½-inch dice

½ pound plum tomatoes, seeded & cut into ½-inch dice

4 boneless skinless chicken breast halves (about 5 ounces each), cut into ¾-inch-wide diagonal strips

½ cup frozen tiny peas, thawed

2 ounces cooked ham, cut into ¼-inch dice

1 tablespoon fresh lemon juice, or to taste

Salt & freshly ground pepper

Hot cooked white rice, for serving

1 tablespoon minced fresh flat-leaf parsley

TARRAGON ROASTED CHICKEN

Serves 4

NOTHING SATISFIES MORE THAN A
PERFECTLY ROASTED CHICKEN. BESIDES THE WAY ALL THE
HERBS AND VEGETABLES ENHANCE
THE FLAVOR OF THE CHICKEN, THE GREAT THING HERE IS
THAT EVERYTHING IS COOKED AT THE
SAME TIME. SO ONCE EVERYTHING GOES INTO THE OVEN,
YOU CAN SIT AND RELAX.

LEMON BUTTER

¼ cup (½ stick) unsalted butter

1 tablespoon minced fresh
flat-leaf parsley

1 teaspoon minced fresh
tarragon

½ teaspoon grated lemon zest

1 (3- to 3½-pound) chicken

1 lemon, cut into 8 wedges

2 fresh tarragon sprigs

2 bay leaves

Salt & freshly ground pepper

8 carrots, halved lengthwise &
cut into 2-inch lengths

1 pound small red potatoes,
quartered

1½ cups diced rutabaga (1-inch)

2 parsnips, cut into 2-inch
lengths

6 shallots, peeled

1 head garlic, broken into cloves

2 tablespoons butter, melted

1 tablespoon minced fresh parsley

1 tablespoon minced fresh
tarragon

Preheat the oven to 400°F.

Prepare the lemon butter: In a small bowl, mash all the ingredients.

Slide your fingers under the skin of the chicken to separate the skin from the meat. Spread the lemon butter evenly over the meat. Place the lemon wedges, tarragon, and bay leaves in the chicken cavity. Truss the chicken and place on a rack in a roasting pan. Sprinkle with ½ teaspoon salt and ¼ teaspoon pepper.

In a large bowl, toss together the carrots, potatoes, rutabaga, parsnips, shallots, garlic cloves, butter, ¼ teaspoon salt and ¼ teaspoon pepper. Scatter the vegetables under and around the rack.

Roast the chicken, basting with the juices and tossing the vegetables, for 1¼ hours, or until the juices from the thigh run clear when pierced.

Put the chicken on a platter; let rest for 10 minutes. Put the vegetables into a bowl and toss with 1½ teaspoons each parsley and tarragon. Arrange the vegetables around the chicken, sprinkle with the remaining 1½ teaspoons each parsley and tarragon, and serve.

MASHED POTATO STUFFED CHICKEN

MASHED POTATO STUFFING

4 slices bacon, chopped

1 large onion, cut into ¼-inch dice

3 pounds baking potatoes, peeled & cut into ½-inch pieces

1 bay leaf

1 teaspoon salt

¼ teaspoon freshly ground pepper

½ cup chicken broth

1 tablespoon fresh thyme leaves

1 (5-pound) chicken, patted dry

2 tablespoons unsalted butter, at room temperature

Salt & freshly ground pepper

12 shallots

2 teaspoons canola or other vegetable oil

6 slender carrots, cut into 2-inch lengths

4 small turnips, peeled & each cut into 8 wedges

EVERYONE LOVES CHICKEN AND MASHED POTATOES, AND WHEN YOU STUFF THE CHICKEN WITH THE POTATOES, THE RESULT IS EVEN BETTER. THE BACON IN THE MASHED POTATOES ISN'T ESSENTIAL, BUT IT IS ABSOLUTELY DELICIOUS.

Prepare the mashed potato stuffing: Cook the bacon in a large skillet until crisp. Remove and drain on a paper towel–lined plate, leaving the fat in the pan. Add the onion to the skillet and cook, stirring frequently, for 5 minutes, or until softened. Remove from the heat and set aside.

Meanwhile, in a large saucepan, combine the potatoes, bay leaf, and enough cold water to cover and bring to a boil over high heat. Reduce the heat to low, cover, and simmer for 15 minutes, or until the potatoes are tender when pierced with a fork.

Drain the potatoes, return them to the pan, and cook over high heat, shaking the pan, for about 30 seconds, or until any liquid has evaporated. Remove from the heat and discard the bay leaf. Mash the potatoes with the salt and pepper. Gradually add the broth, stirring until well blended. Stir in the cooked onions, bacon, and thyme. Let cool completely.

Preheat oven to 450°F. Set a rack in the lower third of the oven.

Fill the chicken cavity loosely with some of the stuffing. Place the remaining stuffing in a small baking dish, cover, and set aside. Truss the chicken. Rub on all sides with the butter and season with salt and pepper.

Place the chicken breast side down on a rack in a roasting pan. Toss the shallots with the oil in a small bowl and add to the roasting pan.

Roast the chicken for 30 minutes. Turn the chicken breast side up and baste with the pan juices. Arrange the carrots, turnips, celery root, and thyme sprigs around the chicken and season with salt and pepper. Roast the chicken and vegetables, stirring the vegetables and basting the chicken every 15 minutes, for 1 hour longer, or until the juices from the thigh run clear when pierced with a paring knife. About 30 minutes before the chicken is done, put the reserved potato stuffing into the oven and bake for 30 minutes, or until hot.

Cover the roasting pan and let the chicken rest for 10 minutes. Discard the thyme sprigs. Remove the potato stuffing from the chicken and put into a serving bowl.

Transfer the chicken to a cutting board and cut into serving pieces. Arrange on a platter along with the vegetables. Sprinkle with the parsley and serve with the additional stuffing alongside.

2 small celery roots, peeled & each cut into 8 wedges

8 fresh thyme sprigs

Minced fresh flat-leaf parsley, for garnish

ROASTED GLAZED
GAME HENS

2 tablespoons rice vinegar

2 tablespoons soy sauce

2 tablespoons Asian sesame oil

Ground red pepper

2 Cornish game hens (about
1¼ pounds each)

2 garlic cloves, halved

Small watercress sprigs,
for garnish

THESE GAME HENS ARE DARKLY GLAZED
AND HAVE A DEEP, INTENSE FLAVOR. NO ONE BUT YOU WILL
KNOW HOW EASY THEY ARE TO PREPARE.

Preheat the oven to 375°F.

In a large bowl, combine the vinegar, soy sauce, sesame oil, and ground red pepper to taste Add the game hens and turn to coat. Marinate at room temperature for 15 minutes, turning occasionally.

Place the hens breast side up on a rack in a roasting pan. Place 1 garlic clove inside each hen cavity and spoon the marinade inside the cavities. Truss the hens. Roast for 1 hour, basting several times, or until the juices from the thigh run clear when pierced with a paring knife.

To serve, using poultry shears or a large knife, halve each bird lengthwise cutting through the breastbone and down along the backbone. Arrange the game hen halves on a warm serving platter, and garnish with the watercress.

BEVERLY HILLS CHICKEN POT PIE

Serves 6

EVEN IN BEVERLY HILLS, THEY LOVE
COMFORT FOOD. I ENJOYED A TERRIFIC CHICKEN POT
PIE THERE AT A VERY CHIC BISTRO, BUT
SINCE I LIVE SO FAR AWAY, I HAD TO LEARN TO
MAKE IT FOR MYSELF.

BLACK PEPPER PASTRY

1⅓ cups all-purpose flour

½ teaspoon salt

½ teaspoon coarsely cracked
   black pepper

3 tablespoons cold vegetable
   shortening

3 tablespoons cold unsalted
   butter, cut into small pieces

3 to 4 tablespoons ice water

1 large egg beaten with
   1 teaspoon water, for
   egg wash

FILLING

1 (3- to 3½-pound) chicken,
   cut into 8 pieces

6 cups chicken broth

1 medium-size onion, chopped

1 cup chopped celery, including
   some leaves

10 fresh flat-leaf parsley sprigs

1 bay leaf

½ teaspoon each fennel seeds &
   whole black peppercorns

5 tablespoons unsalted butter

Prepare the black pepper pastry: In a food processor, combine the flour, salt, and pepper and pulse until mixed. Distribute the shortening and butter on top of the flour and pulse until the mixture resembles coarse meal. With the machine running, add 3 tablespoons of the water, pulsing just until the dough begins to form a ball, adding up to 1 tablespoon more water if necessary. Shape the dough into a disk, wrap in waxed paper, and refrigerate for at least 30 minutes.

Prepare the filling: In a Dutch oven, combine the chicken, broth, onion, celery, parsley, bay leaf, fennel seeds, and peppercorns and bring to a simmer over medium heat. Simmer for 15 minutes, or until the chicken is almost cooked through. Transfer the chicken to a large bowl and set the pot aside.

When the chicken is cool enough to handle, shred the meat, discarding the skin. Return the bones to the broth and simmer for 30 minutes longer.

Pour the broth through a strainer into a large bowl, pressing on the solids with a wooden spoon. Set aside 2 cups of the broth. (Refrigerate or freeze the remaining broth for another use.)

Preheat the oven to 350°F.

3 tablespoons all-purpose flour

1 teaspoon fresh thyme leaves

½ cup heavy cream

1½ teaspoons fresh lemon juice

¼ teaspoon hot pepper sauce

1 cup minced shallots

1 cup diced carrots (¼-inch)

½ pound shiitake mushrooms, stems removed, briefly rinsed & sliced

½ cup frozen baby peas, thawed

¼ teaspoon salt, or to taste

⅛ teaspoon freshly ground pepper

In a medium-size saucepan, melt 3 tablespoons of the butter over medium heat. Whisk in the flour and thyme and cook, whisking, for 3 minutes, until the roux is very light brown. Gradually whisk in 1½ cups of the reserved broth and the cream. Cook, whisking constantly, until the sauce is thickened and smooth. Stir in the lemon juice and hot pepper sauce. Remove from the heat.

In a large heavy skillet, melt the remaining 2 tablespoons butter over medium heat. Add the shallots and cook, stirring, for 2 minutes. Stir in the carrots, shiitakes, and the remaining ½ cup broth. Increase the heat to medium-high and cook, stirring, for about 10 minutes, or until the carrots are tender and the broth has evaporated. Stir in the chicken, peas, and sauce and season with the salt and pepper. Reduce the heat to medium and cook, stirring, for 2 minutes. Transfer the chicken mixture to a shallow baking dish, approximately 10½ x 1½ inches.

Roll out the black pepper pastry between 2 sheets of lightly floured waxed paper to ⅛-inch thickness. Place on top of the filling, pressing the pastry to the edges of the dish to seal. Brush the pastry with the egg wash, cut a few slits in the top of the pastry, and place on a baking sheet.

Bake for 30 minutes, or until the crust is golden brown. Let stand for 10 minutes before serving.

BULGUR & PINE NUT STUFFED CHICKEN

BULGUR & PINE NUT STUFFING

¼ cup (½ stick) unsalted butter

⅓ cup pine nuts

½ cup chopped red onions

1 cup coarse bulgur, soaked in
    warm water to cover for 5
    minutes, then drained well

1 cup chicken broth

¼ cup minced fresh cilantro

¾ teaspoon ground coriander

½ teaspoon ground allspice

Salt & freshly ground pepper

2 tablespoons unsalted butter

¼ teaspoon ground cinnamon

1 (3- to 3½-pound) chicken,
    patted dry

Salt & freshly ground pepper

1 tablespoon minced fresh
    cilantro

AROMATIC, COMPLEX, AND HEARTY, THIS
DISH HAS GREAT AUTHENTIC MIDDLE EASTERN FLAVOR. IT'S
ESPECIALLY GOOD IN WINTERTIME WHEN
IT WILL WARM UP BOTH YOU AND YOUR KITCHEN.

Prepare the bulgur and pine nut stuffing: In a large skillet, melt the butter over medium heat. Cook the pine nuts for about 5 minutes, or until golden. Transfer to a small bowl; set aside. Add the onions to the skillet and cook, stirring, for 5 minutes, or until golden. Add the bulgur and cook for 1 minute. Stir in the broth, pine nuts, cilantro, coriander, and allspice, and season with salt and pepper. Cook, stirring, for 10 minutes, or until the broth is absorbed. Remove from the heat and cool to room temperature.

Preheat the oven to 400°F. Melt the butter with the cinnamon in a small saucepan. Set aside. Fill the chicken cavity loosely with some bulgur stuffing, placing the remaining stuffing in a small baking dish. Cover and set aside. Truss the chicken. Place the chicken on a rack in a roasting pan, brush with the butter mixture, and sprinkle with salt and pepper.

Roast the chicken, basting often, for 1½ hours, or until the juices run clear when the thigh is pierced with a paring knife. Place the baking dish with the stuffing in the oven for the last 30 minutes.

Let the chicken rest loosely covered, for 10 minutes. Remove the stuffing to a serving bowl and sprinkle with the cilantro. To serve, cut the chicken into pieces and arrange on a platter.

CHICKEN WITH SHIITAKES & RED WINE

Serves 2

QUICKLY BROWN THE INGREDIENTS ON TOP OF THE STOVE, THEN FINISH THE CHICKEN OFF IN THE OVEN WHILE YOU'RE READING A BOOK, OR DOING WHATEVER YOU PLEASE. THIS DISH, MADE JUST FOR TWO, HAS GREAT ROBUST FLAVOR WITHOUT HAVING TO ROAST A WHOLE CHICKEN.

¼ cup all-purpose flour

Salt & freshly ground pepper

1 whole chicken breast (about 1 pound), skin removed & split

2 tablespoons olive oil, preferably extra-virgin

2 small onions, thinly sliced

1 garlic clove, minced

¼ pound shiitake mushrooms, stems removed, briefly rinsed & thinly sliced

½ cup chicken broth

½ cup dry red wine

1 teaspoon fresh thyme leaves

Preheat the oven to 350°F.

On a large plate, combine the flour, ½ teaspoon salt, and ½ teaspoon pepper. Lightly coat the chicken with the flour, shaking off the excess.

In an ovenproof skillet with a lid, just large enough to hold the chicken in a single layer, heat 1 tablespoon of the oil over medium heat. Add the chicken and cook, turning once, for 10 to 12 minutes, or until browned. Remove to a large plate.

Add the onions and the remaining 1 tablespoon oil to the skillet and cook, stirring occasionally, for about 5 minutes, or until the onions are softened. Add the garlic and cook, stirring, for 3 minutes. Add the mushrooms and cook, stirring frequently, for about 4 minutes, or until softened.

Return the chicken to the skillet. Stir in the broth, wine, and thyme, and season with salt and pepper.

Bake, covered, stirring several times, for about 1 hour, or until the chicken is very tender and the juices run clear when the thigh is pierced with a paring knife. Transfer the chicken and mushrooms to a platter and serve hot.

CHICKEN PILAF
WITH ORANGE

Serves 4

THIS PILAF IS TRADITIONALLY SERVED AT
WEDDINGS AND OTHER SPECIAL OCCASIONS IN AFGHANISTAN.
NONE OF THE DIFFERENT SEASONINGS JUMP
OUT AT YOU SEPARATELY, BUT TOGETHER THEY COMBINE
TO CREATE A NEW AND INTRIGUING TASTE.
BLANCHING THE ORANGE ZEST REMOVES SOME OF ITS
BITTERNESS AND GREATLY IMPROVES ITS TEXTURE.

1 whole chicken breast
(about 1 pound)

Zest of 1 large orange, removed
in strips with a vegetable
peeler & cut crosswise into
fine shreds

½ cup cold water

½ cup fresh orange juice

¼ cup (½ stick) unsalted butter

2 tablespoons sugar

¼ teaspoon saffron threads,
crumbled

½ teaspoon rose water (optional)

⅛ teaspoon each ground
cardamom and allspice

2 small red onions, thinly sliced

1 cup basmati rice, rinsed in
a strainer until the water
runs clear & drained

1¼ cups chicken broth

Salt & freshly ground pepper

⅓ cup golden raisins

¼ cup sliced almonds, toasted

2 tablespoons chopped
pistachio nuts

Put the chicken into a large saucepan, add enough cold water to cover, and bring to a boil over high heat. Reduce the heat and simmer for 15 minutes. Remove from the heat and set aside for 20 minutes. Remove the chicken and when cool enough to handle, shred the meat, discarding the skin and bones.

Meanwhile, bring a small saucepan of cold water to a boil over high heat. Put the orange shreds into a small strainer, dip the strainer into the boiling water for about 1 minute, and then rinse under cold running water; repeat twice. Set aside.

In a medium-size saucepan, bring the cold water, orange juice, 1 tablespoon of the butter, and the sugar to a boil over medium-high heat. Add the orange zest, reduce the heat, and simmer for 15 minutes.

With a small strainer, scoop out the zest and set aside. Add the saffron and the rose water, if using, to the syrup and simmer for 3 minutes. Stir in the cardamom and allspice and remove from the heat. Set aside.

In a large saucepan, melt the remaining 3 tablespoons butter over medium heat. Add the onions and cook, stirring, for about 5 minutes,

or until softened. Stir in the rice and half of the orange zest and cook, stirring, for 3 minutes. Stir in the broth and saffron syrup and bring to a boil over high heat. Season with salt and pepper, reduce the heat to low, and cook, covered, for about 25 minutes, or until the rice is tender and all the liquid is absorbed. Remove the pan from heat, stir in the chicken, the remaining orange zest, and the raisins, and let stand, covered, for 5 minutes.

Spoon the pilaf onto a serving platter and sprinkle with the almonds and pistachios. Serve while hot.

CLAY POT CHICKEN WITH OLIVES

Serves 4

CLAY POTS RELEASE THEIR HEAT SLOWLY DURING THE BAKING PROCESS. THEY GRADUALLY GIVE UP THE WATER IN WHICH THEY WERE SOAKED THEREBY MOISTENING THE FOOD AS IT COOKS.

1 (3- to 3½-pound) chicken

Salt & freshly ground pepper

1 navel orange, zest removed in strips (with a vegetable peeler) & orange cut into quarters

1 celery stalk with leaves, cut into 2-inch lengths

8 garlic cloves

8 fresh flat-leaf parsley sprigs

6 fresh thyme sprigs

3 fresh rosemary sprigs

2 bay leaves

1 tablespoon fruity olive oil

10 each brine-cured green & black olives, such as Picholine & Nicoise, halved & pitted

1 cup chicken broth

2 teaspoons arrowroot, dissolved in 2 tablespoons cold water

Soak the clay pot top and bottom in cold water to cover for at least 15 minutes; drain.

Sprinkle the chicken cavity with salt and pepper. Place half the orange zest, the orange quarters, celery, 4 garlic cloves, 4 parsley sprigs, 4 thyme sprigs, 2 rosemary sprigs, and 1 bay leaf into the cavity; truss. Place the chicken in the pot; rub with the oil and season with salt and pepper. Distribute the remaining orange zest, 4 garlic cloves, 2 thyme sprigs, 1 rosemary sprig, bay leaf, and olives around the chicken, and add the broth. Cover the pot and place in the center of the cold oven.

Turn the oven on to 450°F and bake the chicken for 70 minutes. Remove from the oven. Remove everything from the pot except the chicken. Strain the liquid into a small saucepan, reserving the olives and garlic. Return the clay pot to the oven and bake, uncovered, for 15 to 25 minutes longer to brown the skin. Skim the fat from the pan liquid. Stir the arrowroot mixture into the juices. Cook, stirring, over medium heat, for about 2 minutes, or until slightly thickened. Keep warm.

To serve, cut the chicken into serving pieces, arrange on a platter, and scatter the olives and garlic cloves on top. Serve the sauce alongside.

WEIGHTS

Ounces and Pounds	Metric Equivalent
1/4 ounce	7 grams
1/3 ounce	10 g
1/2 ounce	14 g
1 ounce	28 g
1 1/2 ounces	42 g
1 3/4 ounces	50 g
2 ounces	57 g
3 ounces	85 g
3 1/2 ounces	100 g
4 ounces (1/4 pound)	114 g
6 ounces	170 g
8 ounces (1/2 pound)	227 g
9 ounces	250 g
16 ounces (1 pound)	464 g

TEMPERATURE

°F (Fahrenheit)	°C (Centigrade or Celsius)
32 (water freezes)	0
200	95
212 (water boils)	100
250	120
275	135
300 (slow oven)	150
325	160
350 (moderate oven)	175
375	190
400 (hot oven)	205
425	220
450 (very hot oven)	232
475	245
500 (extremely hot oven)	260

LIQUID MEASURES

tsp.: teaspoon / Tbs.: tablespoon

Spoons and Cups	Metric Equivalents
1/4 tsp.	1.23 milliliters
1/2 tsp.	2.5 ml
3/4 tsp.	3.7 ml
1 tsp.	5 ml
1 dessertspoon	10 ml
1 Tbs. (3 tsp.)	15 ml
2 Tbs. (1 ounce)	30 ml
1/4 cup	60 ml
1/3 cup	80 ml
1/2 cup	120 ml
2/3 cup	160 ml
3/4 cup	180 ml
1 cup (8 ounces)	240 ml
2 cups (1 pint)	480 ml
3 cups	720 ml
4 cups (1 quart)	1 liter
4 quarts (1 gallon)	3.75 liters

LENGTH

U.S. Measurements	Metric Equivalent
1/8 inch	3 mm
1/4 inch	6 mm
3/8 inch	1 cm
1/2 inch	1.2 cm
3/4 inch	2 cm
1 inch	2.5 cm
1 1/4 inches	3.1 cm
1 1/2 inches	3.7 cm
2 inches	5 cm
3 inches	7.5 cm
4 inches	10 cm
5 inches	12.5 cm

APPROXIMATE EQUIVALENTS

1 kilo is slightly more than 2 pounds
1 liter is slightly more than 1 quart
1 meter is slightly over 3 feet
1 centimeter is approximately 3/8 inch

WINTER CHICKEN

INDEX